New Deal Adobe

THE CIVILIAN CONSERVATION CORPS AND
THE RECONSTRUCTION OF MISSION LA PURÍSIMA
1934-1942

Christine E. Savage

FITHIAN PRESS · SANTA BARBARA · 1991

For *Lex Palmer,*
who introduced me to the
history and serenity of Mission La Purísima,

and for the memory of
Mell Callan,
who wanted the story of the CCC
at La Purísima to be told.

Design and typography by Jim Cook/Santa Barbara

Published by Fithian Press
Post Office Box 1525, Santa Barbara, California 93120

LIBRARY OF CONGRESS CATALOGING-IN-PUBLICATION DATA
Savage, Christine E., 1949-
    New Deal adobe: the Civilian Conservation Corps and the
reconstruction of Mission La Purísima, 1934-1942 / Christine E.
Savage.
        p.   cm.
    Includes bibliographical references.
    ISBN 0-931832-75-6
    1. Mission La Purísima Concepción (Calif.)   2. Civilian
Conservation Corps (U.S.)   3. Spanish mission buildings—
California—Lompoc Region—Conservation and restoration.
4. Indians of North America—California—Lompoc Region—
Architecture—Conservation and restoration.   5. Lompoc Region
(Calif.)—History.   I. Title.
F869.M65S28   1990
979.4'91—dc20   90-14051
                                                           CIP

Contents

Preface 7
Introduction 9

1. The Early Mission 11
Spanish Days • The Mission Ruins

2. The Civilian Conservation Corps 15
Roosevelt's New Deal • Creation of the CCC • La Purísima Rescued

3. Camp Beginnings 23
CCC Camp Established • The Enrollees • Gilbert Ballesterose • Frank
Hines • Robert Zaragoza • Black Enrollees • CCC Camp Food •
Community Relations • Ed Negus • Negus's Employment Interview

4. Project Management 45
Advisory Committee Established • The Construction Foremen • Camp
Hierarchy • Handling the Crews

5. Preserve or Rebuild? 54
Hageman's Research • Architect's Background • The Preserve or
Rebuild Dilemma • Professional Consultants • Advisory Committee's
Recommendations

6. From the Ground Up 62
Excavation of Ruins • Elevated Foundations • The First Adobe Bricks
• Rebuilding Begins • Making and Laying the Adobe Bricks • The
Pugmill • Burning the Tiles • Raymond Ellis • The Abitudobe
Experiment • Steel Reinforced Concrete

7. "Spike" Camps 80
   Fire Suppression Work • The Jolon Fire • Morro Bay Spike Camp

8. Camp Changes 84
   CCC Camp Revamped • The Lompoc SCS Camp • The Twin
   Camps' Routine

9. Camp Life 95
   Leave Passes, AWOL, and Desertion • Payday • CCC Camp
   Newspapers • The Motor Pool • Harry Davis

10.The Mission Takes Shape 105
   Redwood Beams • Roof Construction • Plastering the Walls • Color
   Pigments • Woodwork and Hardware Handmade • Furniture Making
   • Leo Mandeville

11. The Site Refined 119
   Residence Building Dedicated and State Park Opened • Water
   Structures Restored • Gardens • Horticulturist's Background •
   Seymour Adler

12.Other Mission Buildings 131
   Church and Cemetery • Campañario • Shops and Quarters Building

13. Camp Recreation 137
   The Boxing Ring • The Barracks Poker Game • Liquor • Hazing •
   Captain Tornell's Garden • CCC Education at La Purísima • The Blue
   Banner

14.Final Work 149
   Hageman Relieved • WPA Artists • Old Mission Days • Camp Cooke
   • Hageman After La Purísima • La Purísima Today

   For Further Reading 162

Preface

An African proverb says when an old man dies, a library burns to the ground. The tradition of remembering events through oral narration is older than writing. In producing this history, I have drawn from both methods, allowing the written records to corroborate and supplement the remembrances of Civilian Conservation Corps enrollees at the Mission La Purísima reconstruction project.

During the spring and summer of 1989, Prelado de los Tesoros, the docent organization at La Purísima Mission State Historic Park, asked me to research and write about the reconstruction of the mission in the 1930s by the Civilian Conservation Corps. From the start, they knew interviews with the remaining living enrollees would be the focus of the work, and provided me with excellent resources to begin the joyful task of talking to old men with fond memories. CCC veteran interviewees were selected based on the variety of jobs each man performed at the mission site. Primary sources for written records were found in three places: the La Purísima Mission Archives with its nearby Docent Research Library, the Community Development and Conservation Collection housed in the Department of Special Collections in the Library at the University of California at Santa Barbara, and the Presidio Research Center at El Presídio de Santa Bárbara State Historic Park.

In some instances, it was not possible to back up a verbal account with historical documents. For this reason, the reader should keep in mind that an oral history interview is someone's memory of an event, not an exact representation of that event. It is highly personal, but often more enriching and always more lively than the written accounts. In his book *Envelopes of Sound,* historian Ronald J. Grele described the oral history interview as a "conversational narrative: conversational because of the relationship of interviewer and interviewee, and narrative because of the form of exposition—the telling of a tale." It is also very often the most enjoyable part of historical research.

Grateful acknowledgements must be made for the help and support provided to me by the Oral History Committee of Prelado de los Tesoros, and La Purísima Mission State Historic Park Superintendent Russell Guiney. At UCSB's Special Collections, I received unparalleled assistance from Roseanne Barker, curator of the Community Development and Conservation Collection. Cathy Rudolph, director of Research and Interpretation in the Presidio Research Center at El Presídio de Santa Bárbara State Historic Park, was also especially helpful. My classmate in UCSB's Public Historical Studies graduate program, Drew Johnson, provided excellent editorial insights.

My most glowing gratitude must be extended to the men I interviewed: National Park Service Construction Foreman Edward Negus, and Civilian Conservation Corps Veteran Enrollees Seymour Adler, Gilbert Ballesterose, Harry Davis, Ray Ellis, Frank Hines, Leo Mandeville, and Robert Zaragoza. They were the best of history teachers.

CHRISTINE E. SAVAGE
Goleta, California

Introduction

Writers of popular travel literature regard Mission La Purísima as the "Williamsburg of the West"[1] because it is the most historically accurate reconstruction on the West Coast. In his book *Preservation Comes of Age* (1981), nationally recognized preservation historian Charles B. Hosmer, Jr., wrote, "From the beginning the Purísima project could be compared in scale and thoroughness with the most involved restorations in the East—even Colonial Williamsburg."[2] The meticulous and expensive reconstruction of eighteenth-century Williamsburg in Virginia was privately financed with Rockefeller Foundation funds beginning in 1926. Mission La Purísima had to wait a little longer to enjoy an unusual confluence of events which enabled it to rise for a second time from its adobe ruins. The Great Depression of the 1930s forced bold societal changes, among them Franklin Roosevelt's New Deal which gave birth to the Civilian Conservation Corps, or CCC. The young, unemployed, unskilled men of the CCC rebuilt La Purísima under the direction of the National Park Service. Most of the methods and tools they used were the same as those of the unskilled Chumash Indians who constructed the mission the first two times under the direction of the Franciscan padres.

This is an account of what it was like for both unskilled laborers and trained professionals finally to find a job during the Depression, to be able to send money home to a struggling family, to live in an army camp, to work with different kinds of people, and to labor under the Santa Barbara County sunshine to reproduce a group of buildings of historical significance. With a few notable exceptions, every bit of construction at the mission site was done as authentically as possible, with many of the same hand tools duplicating the same images as the original. It took the CCC men about as much time to reconstruct the site as it had originally taken the Chumash Indians under the direction of Spanish Franciscan padres.

---

1. William Wilson Robinson, *Panorama: A Picture History of Southern California,* Title Insurance and Trust Company (Los Angeles, 1953), p. 60.
2. Charles B. Hosmer, Jr., *Preservation Comes of Age,* Vol. II, University Press of Virginia (Charlottesville, 1981), p. 426.

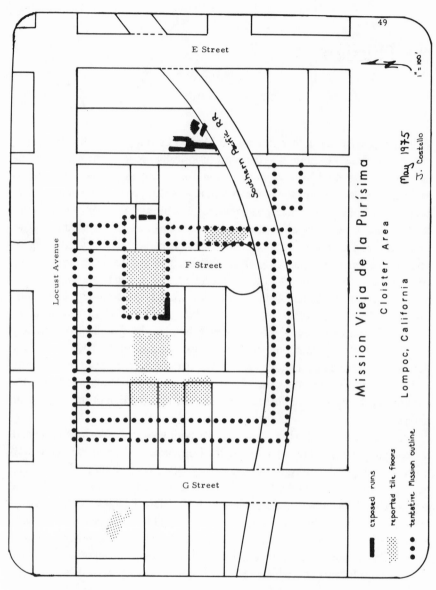

The quadrangle plan of the first Mission La Purísima superimposed on a map of the town of Lompoc. Note the way F Street cuts through the church building in the mission complex. From the 1975 archaeological survey by Julia Costello. (Reprinted from Pacific Coast Archaeological Society Quarterly, Vol. II, No. 2 [April 1975]; courtesy Pacific Coast Archaeological Society.)

1. The Early Mission

Spanish Days

Founded on December 8, 1787, by Franciscan Padre Presidente Fermín Francisco de Lasuén, *Misión La Purísima Concepción de María Santísima* (Mission of the Immaculate Conception of Most Holy Mary) was first located on the south side of what is now the town of Lompoc, California. The buildings were constructed by christianized Chumash Indians who were directed by Franciscan padres. The Franciscans designed it in the traditional mission quadrangle form, and it prospered spiritually and temporally for twenty-five years before being destroyed by an earthquake in 1812. The padres relocated to La Cañada de Los Berros (Canyon of the Watercresses) four miles away in 1813, the present site of La Purísima, and began a second construction program. This time the quadrangle design was not used and the buildings were erected in a linear pattern inside the narrow valley. La Purísima is the only mission in the Alta California chain of twenty-one to break from the customary quadrangle design.

Most adult Chumash in the vicinity of La Purísima had died of white-men's diseases or had been converted to Christianity by 1805.[1] Padre Mariano Payeras, the driving force behind La Purísima's success, died in 1823. In 1824, La Purísima was the site of the largest Indian revolt in the Alta California chain of missions, which involved more than four hundred mission and non-mission Indians.[2] The Mexican government secularized all the missions in 1834, beginning a process that appropriated mission lands and allowed their furnishings to be plundered by local residents. Catholic services ceased to be held at La Purísima after 1836, and in 1845 it was sold at auction for $1,110.[3] The surrounding lands became Rancho La Purísima and the deteriorating buildings were used as dwellings and storehouses by successive landowners. The roof tiles, pilfered by nearby residents in the subsequent decades, exposed the adobe walls to the elements and eroded them to piles of rubble.

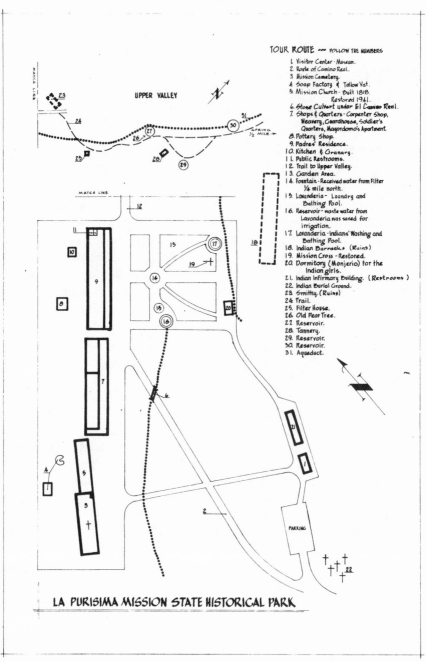

TOUR ROUTE ∞ FOLLOW THE NUMBERS

1. Visitor Center - Museum.
2. Route of Camino Real.
3. Mission Cemetery.
4. Soap Factory & Tallow Vat.
5. Mission Church - Built 1818.
   Restored 1941.
6. Stone Culvert under El Camino Real.
7. Shops & Quarters - Carpenter Shop,
   Weavery, Guardhouse, Soldier's
   Quarters, Majordomo's Apartment.
8. Pottery Shop.
9. Padres' Residence.
10. Kitchen & Granary.
11. Public Restrooms.
12. Trail to Upper Valley.
13. Garden Area.
14. Fountain - Received water from Filter
    ¼ mile north.
15. Lavanderia - Laundry and
    Bathing Pool.
16. Reservoir - waste water from
    Lavanderia was saved for
    irrigation.
17. Lavanderia - Indians' Washing and
    Bathing Pool.
18. Indian Barracks (Ruins)
19. Mission Cross - Restored.
20. Dormitory (Monjerio) for the
    Indian girls.
21. Indian Infirmary Building. (Restrooms)
22. Indian Burial Ground.
23. Smithy. (Ruins)
24. Trail.
25. Filter House.
26. Old Pear Tree.
27. Reservoir.
28. Tannery.
29. Reservoir.
30. Reservoir.
31. Aqueduct.

UPPER VALLEY

MATCH LINE

MATCH LINE

SPRING
½ MILE

PARKING

LA PURISIMA MISSION STATE HISTORICAL PARK

An early 1950s state park brochure showing all buildings reconstructed up to that time. [MISSION LA PURISIMA ARCHIVES]

Local high school student, D.A. Brickey, visited ruins (ca. 1930). Local residents commonly played, picnicked, and camped among the crumbling adobe walls and pillars, prompting the concern of property owner Union Oil Company to remove loose roof tiles to prevent injuries. This practice unwittingly contributed to the destruction of the mission. [MISSION LA PURISIMA ARCHIVES]

The Mission Ruins

By the turn of the century, Californians were reexamining their Spanish heritage and taking a new interest in the crumbling mission structures. Led by groups such as the Landmarks Club of California and the Native Sons of the Golden West, preservation of the missions became an important issue. By 1902, La Purísima was "the most desolate ruin of all" in the assessment of *Ramona* author Helen Hunt Jackson,4 and the possibility of resurrecting it a second time was very dim.

Ownership of the property eventually came into the hands of the Union Oil Company in 1903, and its officials became interested in encouraging a movement toward restoring the padres' residence building with private capital. In 1905, they deeded the property to the Landmarks Club of California with the provision that the Club would provide $1,500 to preserve and repair the building. The Club was unable to raise the funds and the title reverted back to The Union Oil Company.5 The action of winter rains on the exposed adobe caused disintegration of the ruins to become increasingly rapid in the following decades, but no private or public funds could be found to preserve them. But by the 1930s, a combination of events took place that eventually restored Mission La Purísima.

---

1. Zephryn Engelhardt, *Misión La Concepción Purísima de María Santísima,* Mission Santa Barbara (Santa Barbara, 1932), p. 23; John R. Johnson, *Chumash Social Organization: An Ethnohistoric Perspective,* Ph.D. Dissertation in Anthropology, University of California at Santa Barbara (1988), p. 136.
2. James A. Sandos, "Levantamiento! The 1824 Chumash Uprising," *The Californians,* Vol. 5, No. 1 (Jan.-Feb. 1987), p. 9.
3. Engelhardt, op. cit., p. 65.
4. *Glimpses of California and the Missions,* Little Brown and Company (Boston, 1903), p. 93.
5. Richard S. Whitehead, ed., *An Archaeological and Restoration Study of Misión La Purísima Concepción—Reports Written for the National Park Service by Fred C. Hageman and Russell C. Ewing,* Santa Barbara Trust for Historic Preservation (Santa Barbara, 1980), p. 221.

2. The Civilian Conservation Corps

Roosevelt's New Deal

After Franklin Delano Roosevelt was inaugurated President on March 4, 1933, he put through a series of swift executive and legislative enactments known as the New Deal to help alter the adverse economic and social effects of the Great Depression. The Civilian Conservation Corps was one program in which he took a personal interest from the start, and it became the most popular program of the New Deal. The CCC men appealed to an enduring American mystique with their work in the nation's remaining forest frontiers. In his book *The Civilian Conservation Corps, 1933-1942: A New Deal Case Study* (1967), historian John A. Salmond wrote, "More than any other New Deal agency it bore the personal stamp of President Roosevelt."[1] In his inaugural address, FDR said, "Our greatest primary task is to put people to work,"[2] and that goal became the foundation of nine years of CCC productivity.

Creation of the CCC

Originally called the Emergency Conservation Work Act, or ECW, the Civilian Conservation Corps functioned as a public employment program from April 5, 1933, to June 30, 1942.[3] It employed more than three million Depression-era men. Ten percent of CCC enrollees were black, special programs were created for Native Americans, and separate camps were established for veterans of World War I. With a speed typical of early New Deal programs, the first CCC camp was established on April 17, 1933, at Luray, Virginia, and named Camp Roosevelt.[4]

Administratively, the CCC was a joint effort among offices within the Departments of War, Labor, Agriculture, and the Interior. The Labor Department selected enrollees and the War Department operated the camps through the U.S. Army. The Departments of Agriculture and Interior directed most of the work projects in the camps. The Office of Education directed educational activities, but

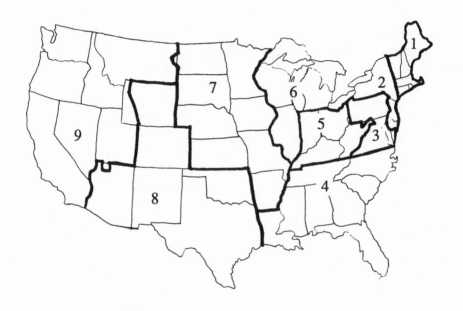

Nine corps areas of the Civilian Conservation Corps.

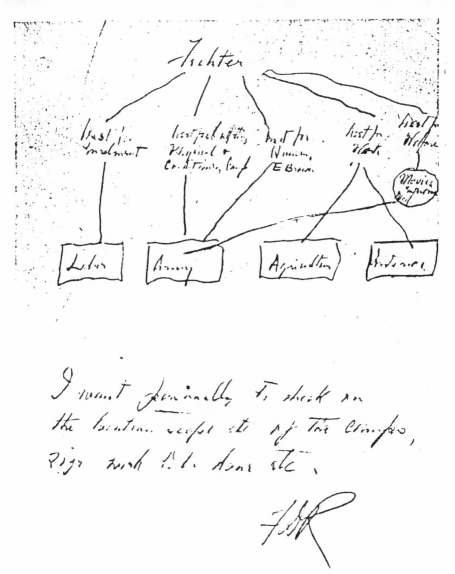

President Roosevelt's diagram of CCC organization. Note FDR spelled Fechner's name incorrectly.

these efforts were controlled by the Army in the camps. Although the administrative organization was complex, it functioned surprisingly well. This was partly due to FDR's personal support, but was mostly the result of the administrative skills of Robert Fechner, a prominent labor leader whom the President chose as director of the CCC.

Over the nine-year existence of the CCC, an average of 1,500 camps consisting of approximately 200 men each were located in all parts of the nation, but camps were more common in the western states where there were many national forests and national parks. The country was divided into nine corps areas which were subdivided into districts.5 The final organizational unit was the camp which was usually commanded by a captain or first lieutenant in the Regular or Reserve Army. This officer was in charge of camp operation and enrollee welfare.

Work projects were the responsibility of the "technical services" personnel from various government departments, usually the Department of Agriculture or Interior, who planned and directed CCC activities. Seventy-five percent of camp projects were supervised by the Department of Agriculture, and over half of these were operated by Agriculture's subdivision, the Forest Service. Other Department of Agriculture agencies administering camps included the Soil Conservation Service, the Bureau of Agricultural Engineering, and the Tennessee Valley Authority. A large number of the remaining camps were administered by the National Park Service, a division of the Department of the Interior, which was the controlling agency at Mission La Purísima's reconstruction site. Many more work projects were carried out under the direction of state park organizations. At La Purísima, the California State Park authority owned the land and provided critical input into the project since it was to become the maintaining agency after the mission was rebuilt.

CCC enrollees signed on for six-month hitches, and could re-enroll three times, for a maximum of two years of service. The daily routine in a CCC camp called for an eight-hour work day, five days per week. For their work, enrollees received $30 per month, $25 of which was automatically sent home to the enrollee's family in the form of a U.S Treasury check, leaving him $5 per month spending money. Education and recreation were offered at each camp, although the quality of these activities varied considerably from camp to camp. In all but the most isolated camps, enrollees were able to visit nearby towns on weekends.

Nationally, the average enrollee was a twenty-year-old Caucasian, equally likely to be from an urban or a rural background, who had never held a regular full-time job prior to entering the CCC. He came from a household of six children where the father was employed, and joined the CCC primarily to help his family financially. He had an eighth grade education, weighed 147 pounds, and stood five feet, eight inches in height. The average enrollee stayed in the CCC for ten months.6

The CCC had two major objectives: to provide economic support for enrollees and their families, and to protect and enhance natural resources through reforestation, fire control, soil conservation, development of outdoor recreation areas, and preservation of historic sites. For many families, the CCC allotment was the only source of income, and the program touched the lives of as many as two-and-a-half

Conservation Corps Camps.

million families. The value of CCC conservation work paid for the original costs of the program several times over. The CCC also contributed significantly to the physical health, work habits, and self-esteem of most enrollees, and played an important role in preparing them for effective military service in World War II. The CCC brought the idea of conservation to the American people, which had consequences far beyond the work they actually performed.

However, the CCC did not do all things well. Education of enrollees, many of whom quit high school to join, received little emphasis. The inadequate effort in this area can be traced to Director Fechner's, President Roosevelt's, and the Army's view that this was not a principal objective. Education and sometimes even vocational training were often seen as interfering with the major goal of the work projects. Fechner publicly opposed expansion of the camp educational programs, saying that an enrollee's preparation for the future was an "incidental objective."[7] At La Purísima's CCC camp, this lack of emphasis on education translated into a lackadaisical attitude about formal instruction among the enrollees, resulting in sporadic attendance at the optional classes.

Throughout the Depression years, enrollment in CCC camps fluctuated, but averaged about 300,000 nationally. Registration peaked in August 1935 at 520,000. Because of the necessary housing and food expenses, the annual cost per enrollee was approximately $1,000, considerably higher than other work relief agencies of the New Deal. The Works Progress Administration (WPA) had a yearly cost of $800 for each worker, and at the National Youth Administration (NYA) the cost was between $400 and $700 per worker per year.[8] In spite of its relative costliness, the CCC enjoyed a broad base of public support throughout its nine-year history and was praised by both parties in Congress. At one point, one out of every twenty youths over seventeen years old entered the CCC.[9]

The CCC was terminated because of expanding job opportunities during World War II. Despite its tremendous contributions to the nation's natural resources, the CCC was viewed by both Congress and the American people as a temporary relief agency, and it never overcame that image.[10] Consequently, as the economy improved and World War II captured the nation's attention and resources, the CCC was dismantled without opposition. The legacy the men of the CCC left in the nation's forests, parks, agricultural areas, and historic sites is immeasurable. Mission La Purísima is part of that legacy.

La Purísima Rescued

An unusual conjunction of events occurred allowing the second resurrection of Mission La Purísima. While driving south along the California coast in April

1934, CCC Camp Inspector Phillip T. Primm came upon the mission ruins by following an auto club road sign as he was leaving the town of Lompoc, Santa Barbara County, California.[11] He suggested to the staff at the National Park Service Regional Office in San Francisco that the site would be an appropriate choice for a CCC camp. Primm began working with L. Deming Tilton, chief planner of Santa Barbara County, to examine the possibility of Santa Barbara County obtaining the property from Union Oil Company in order to begin work on the mission.[12] National Park Service Staff Architect Frederick C. Hageman described the next steps taken to develop the reconstruction project.

> A certain number of CCC camps were allotted to the National Park Service to develop national, state, county, and municipal parks. In 1934, when it became evident that one of these camps could be stationed in Santa Barbara County, the possibility of restoring La Purísima brought immediate action to provide sufficiently large acreage.
>
> By deed of gift, titles to the mission ruins were transfered to Santa Barbara County by the Catholic Church and the Union Oil Company. The County and State jointly purchased additional land, for a total of 507 acres. This was then deeded in its entirety to the State of California, Division of State Parks, and was named La Purísima State Historic Monument. The State Park Commission requested the National Park Service to establish a CCC Camp at the site and to undertake restoration of the mission buildings, in cooperation with the State Division of Parks.[13]

1. John A. Salmond, *The Civilian Conservation Corps, 1933-1942: A New Deal Case Study,* Duke University Press (Durham, North Carolina, 1967), p. 6.
2. Franklin D. Roosevelt, *Inaugural Address, March 4, 1933,* U.S. Government Printing Office, General Services Administration (Washington, D.C., 1933).
3. Salmond, op. cit., pp. 31, 217.
4. Ibid., p. 31.
5. Leslie Alexander Lacy, *The Soil Soldiers,* Chilton Book Company (Radnor, Pennsylvania, 1976), p. 17.
6. Kenneth Holland and Frank Ernest Hill, *Youth in the CCC,* American Council on Education (Washington, D.C., 1942), p. 58.
7. United States Congress. House Committee on Labor. *Hearings on H.R. 6180, A Bill to Make the CCC a Permanent Agency,* 75th Congress, 1st Session, April 14-15, 1937. U.S. Government Printing Office, General Services Administration (Washington, D.C., 1937).
8. Salmond, op. cit., p. 128.

9. United States Department of Labor. *Annual Report of the Secretary of Labor, Fiscal Year Ended June 30, 1938.* U.S. Government Printing Office, General Services Administration (Washington, D.C., 1938).

10. Salmond, op. cit., pp. 218-219.

11. Charles B. Hosmer, Jr., *Preservation Comes of Age,* Vol. II, University Press of Virginia (Charlottesville, North Carolina, 1981), p. 428.

12. Ibid., p. 528.

13. Frederick C. Hageman and Olaf T. Hagen, *Mission La Purísima Concepción—A Glance Through its History and the Story of its Restoration,* National Park Service, United States Department of the Interior (undated), Mission La Purísima Archives, Lompoc, California, p. 14.

3. Camp Beginnings

CCC Camp Established

CCC Company 1951, called the Santa Rosa Camp, was first organized at La Purísima by Regular Army Captain Ben O. Badgley on July 23, 1934, with a cadre of seventeen men taken from Camp Bates Canyon and Camp Cuyama.[1] No buildings had yet been constructed, so the camp was set up in five army tents, eight men to a tent, located around an old pepper tree which stood near the ruin of the padre's residence building. On August 1, the camp was formally occupied by the main body of CCC enrollees, thirty-five more tents were set up, and field work began on August 2.[2]

On August 8, Dr. Owen C. Coy of the State Historical Commission led a meeting at the mission site to plan the work program for at least six months.[3] Most of the people at this first meeting would later become the La Purísima Advisory

Early days of Santa Rosa Camp (1934). Note the mission ruins behind the tents.
[MISSION LA PURISIMA ARCHIVES]

Committee. They decided that the first step should be an archaeological survey of the site under the supervision of a trained architect. In September, members of the State Park Commission, led by chairman and *Oakland Tribune* editor, Joseph Knowland, met with Deming Tilton and other officials of Santa Barbara County to make some quick decisions. Since Emergency Conservation Work Act (CCC) projects could only operate on state-owned land, the Commission agreed unanimously to put up half the funds needed to purchase five hundred acres.[4] With the state's acquisition of the property, the CCC work project was guaranteed. Two months after CCC Company 1951 was organized, Regular Army Captain Stewart C. Clinton took over command, and remained in charge until December, 1935.[5]

The Santa Rosa Camp encountered many hardships during the first few months of its existence, especially lack of water. There were no wells, no cleared springs, and no water systems near the camp, so all water had to be transported in an old tank hauled by an Army truck. No mess hall had been constructed as yet, and the food had to be prepared in one of the tents or over open fires. The CCC enrollees used portable Army mess kits and sat around the grounds while eating their food.[6] They had to be admonished to stop carving their initials on the mission ruins.[7]

A short time later, four wooden buildings were constructed or moved in from other locations. One of the constructed buildings served as offices for both the Army and the Technical Services personnel from the National Park Service, as well as living quarters for members of the staff. A large mess hall was then erected in front of the ruin of the padres' residence building.[8] These CCC buildings were later moved to the hill overlooking the mission site.

The Enrollees

Most of the men who rebuilt Mission La Purísima came from southern California, with some from out-of-state. Throughout the duration of the project, the largest enrollee demographic group came from the City of Los Angeles.[9] Many were tough street boys of Mexican-American background who had seen the worst of Depression-era urban poverty before coming to the regular meals and discipline of the CCC work experience. From the earliest days of the tent camp, one of the Army sergeants kept a boxing ring set up. Whenever there was a squabble among the men, the disputing parties were placed in the ring to settle it after the work day ended. This and other features of the CCC experience changed the young men's lives in ways none would forget. Away from home for the first time, experiencing

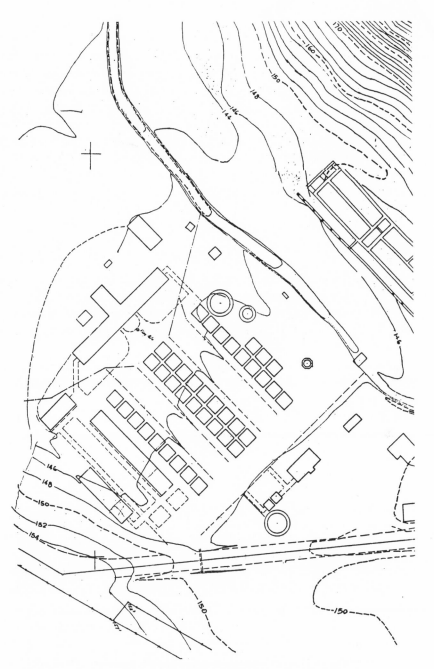

Map of tent city located east of residence building in today's Mission garden.
[MISSION LA PURISIMA ARCHIVES]

Santa Rosa Camp Tent City in front of mission ruins. Note the few standing corridor pillars and, behind them, trenching excavation (1935). [MISSION LA PURISIMA ARCHIVES]

the unsettling life of Army camp, the new Camp 1951 enrollees found an adventure they could recall vividly fifty years later.

GILBERT BALLESTEROSE
Not all enrollees sought CCC employment because they were desperate for work. Some needed to escape an unhappy home at a tender age, or wanted to get away from unfulfilling scholastic pursuits in high school. Many enrollees who looked older than the minimum age requirement of seventeen years lied to get into the CCC to find adventure and a new home. Gilbert Ballesterose was such an enrollee.

> I was fifteen in 1936 and having problems in the tenth grade at Santa Barbara High School. While working picking peas and tomatoes, I heard about the CCC from some of the other workers. So I went to the Santa Barbara County Courthouse and found out it was run by the Army and I could get $30 a month and they gave us uniforms and took care of our

Truck driver Manuel Gilbert Ballesterose, age 18, with a National Park Service Dodge truck (1938). [COURTESY OF MR. BALLESTEROSE]

medical and so forth. I knew I was too young, but I got an application and went home and filled it out. I never told my mother what I had in mind. There was a little old man who lived in a shed behind our house and I brought him a half-quart of wine. I got him to sign my application as guardian. I had a very domineering mother, an oldtime discipline parent. And my stepfather wouldn't tell me anything, so I wasn't very happy. So I went ahead and joined the CCC.

They told me to meet the truck to be picked up in front of my house at 11:00. If I wasn't there, they were going to pass me by. Nobody guessed that I was only fifteen, but we all looked young on that truck that day, so maybe some others were lying, too. That morning, I told my mother what I had done, and to my surprise, she seemed relieved. No tears, no sad goodbyes or anything. When the truck arrived full of hollering guys, I ran out of the house with glee and we took off. I was processed at a camp in San Bernardino, where loads of trucks were bringing in and taking out boys everyday.

From there I was sent to CCC Camp Hawkins Bar operated by the National Forest Service. It was near the town of Salyer, located right on the Trinity River in Northern California. Beautiful, beautiful, beautiful country. Salyer was nothing but a post office, a beer joint and the sheriff's home. We built bridges, roads, and trails and fought fires. There were a lot of boys from San Francisco and Oakland in that camp, lots of fishermen's sons and they were tough guys. There were even some hillbillies who had never worn shoes in their lives.

It was a huge camp and it was always a mystery to me how they kept peace among such a large group of guys. But times were hard during the Depression and these guys knew that they had to behave themselves to make money to send home. We all had something to do and they trained me to drive a truck so I could get supplies at Eureka, about two hundred miles away. Some of the roads up there weren't really roads and it was pretty difficult to drive a loaded truck. But I loved that life and appreciated being there. Some guys felt like they had to be there and were argumentative. But I loved every second of it![10]

Ballesterose was given the nickname "Bali" by the other boys in camp. He kept re-enrolling at Hawkins Bar until he reached the end of his maximum two-year stay in the CCC in 1938. He managed to stay in the Corps even longer by transferring to the La Purísima Camp, located in a different CCC regional district, where he was enrolled as a new man. The company commander allowed the transfer so Ballesterose could be closer to his Santa Barbara home. Perhaps because he was younger than most of the other enrollees, he didn't smoke, drink, box, or play poker in the barracks. In the evenings, he usually spent his time with a Zane Grey novel.[11]

I never had been to Lompoc or heard of La Purísima. I came down on a freight train and they left me off at Surf on a Friday. After being among those redwood trees, La Purísima seemed so dry. Walt Stewart got me started driving a truck, and I became the person who drove to the oil shipping storage area at Avila to get the camp's oil supply. We oiled our barracks twice a month and that oil also killed every flea and tick. But I also got to work on the mission buildings, too. I used to like to work with the adobe mud and stomp around in the mudpits because it was cool. Some guys used to even put it on their faces because we thought it was good for the complexion.

I remember we got the clay for the roof and floor tiles from someplace other than where the adobe earth came from, and after they baked those tiles, they were like iron. At first I just thought it was all too much work, but then I saw the beauty of it coming up as the mission got built. We were doing something that would last. Today I take my grandchildren there and show them the altar. I used an adze on the wood that got placed on the altar. I remember we tied cut-up pieces of tires around our ankles for protection when we were using the adze.

I had a little piece of every job at La Purísima, even climbed the scaffolding to build the walls. I always tried to sneak in on every job just to be able to say I did it. I even got involved in building the furniture and used to go to Surf to get gallons of salt water to soak the leather they used to tie up the chair joints. We also used sand to soften the leather and age the wood. I even found some pottery when we were excavating the grounds around the mission and the aqueduct. It was really intriguing how that water flowed all through that aqueduct for miles to the mission fountains. Those Franciscans really knew what they were doing.

My years in the Civilian Conservation Corps were the happiest of my life. It taught me discipline and responsibility that I used later in life. And it taught me about adapting. It seems that's what it takes to survive in this world and I became a survivor. I never had any training at home because we had a family of nine. I got my high school equivalency after the war and went to UCLA to get my teacher certification in auto body repair. Maybe it was because I didn't inquire, but I don't remember any educational classes in the La Purísima Camp. I remember getting books from the library, but that's it. Most of the news we got was from the radio.[12]

Ballesterose left the CCC in September 1940, served in the Navy during World War II, and became a baker's apprentice afterward. When he achieved his state teacher's certification, he was hired by the Santa Barbara school system to teach welding and auto body repair. He felt his CCC experiences made him a better instructor to the young boys in his automotive classes.[13]

FRANK HINES

One young man, unlike most of his peers, kept re-enrolling in the CCC in order to complete his education and get a high school diploma. Santa Monica enrollee Franklin Hines worked at a wide variety of jobs at the mission reconstruction project. Coming from a family of four children, Frank was seventeen years old, six-foot-two, and desperate for a job. He had been working with the National

Adobe wall builder Frank Hines, age 20 (1939). [COURTESY ROBERT ZARAGOZA]

Youth Project on the old Santa Monica Airport, keeping the tarmac and landing field clear of brush and weeds.

> The man in charge said, "Frank, why don't you join the CCC? It's a helluva lot better than what you're doing here." He gave me the information necessary to enroll and I was sent to the staging area at Fort MacArthur [in San Pedro] first. There was no training involved. It was simply show up, get on the truck, and you're gone. I had one physical and one typhoid shot. God, we hated those shots. I remember digging ditches at camp with my arm swollen up from the typhoid shot. It was miserable. They gave me a barracks bag and my CCC clothing and then I was put to work.[14]

Enrollees could request a particular camp assignment after processing at Fort MacArthur, but Hines "didn't request anything because I didn't know anything." He served at two other camps before coming to La Purísima, learning surveying procedures at the Ash Mountain CCC Company, Camp Potwisha, in Sequoia National Park.

> I learned quite a bit about plane table surveys and contour mapping. When I first arrived at La Purísima, the project superintendent asked if any of the new men had surveying experience. Of course, I jumped up and said I'd had some at Sequoia. I was put to work first on a two-man survey crew doing topographical mapping of the mission grounds and the water supply system. The other man handled the transit and the plane table, and I was the chain and rod man. We finished it in two weeks.[15]

Hines went on to positions as a plasterer, cook, roof tile layer, and used the adze on wooden beams. Because of his unusual diligence in continuing with classes at camp, Lompoc High School granted him a diploma in June 1940. After the CCC he went into the business of manufacturing wooden interior shutters, room dividers and decorative doors. But that turned out to be a sideline.

> I took my high school diploma and got into Santa Monica City College, and then transferred to UCLA's Theater Arts Department and became an actor. My stage name was Ryan Hayes, and I appeared on stage, screen and television [look for him in the 20th Century Fox film *Bus Stop* with Marilyn Monroe and *Gunsmoke* television reruns]. I would not have been able to complete my education and transfer to UCLA had it not been for the CCC. I started acting in 1951 in the Santa Monica Community Theater group and an agent picked me up, so I began acting professionally.[16]

Hines had very strong memories of camp life at La Purísima.

> Each barracks held twenty single army cots, ten on a side. Most of the boys were from the poorer sections of Los Angeles. Some were boxers who boxed at games held in Pismo Beach to earn some extra money. They taught me to box and I taught them English. They were really tough kids, but they took to camp discipline very well because they didn't want to be kicked out. They took great pride in their work and were proud of what they were doing on the mission. They had been on the streets of east

[31]

L.A., hungry half the time, and to be able to do that kind of work in a place where they could have self-respect was great. It was probably the best thing that ever happened to us.

I went to La Purísima with my friend Jimmy Vasil who later became a school teacher in the Santa Monica school system. We were the only two Anglos in a barracks of Mexican-Americans, and we felt a little odd. Our barracks leader, Philip Brito, gave us a short, emphatic lecture on racial discrimination, and we all got along beautifully after that. Of course, I'd had a year and a half of Spanish in school and that helped a great deal.[17]

Like most enrollees, Frank Hines was just glad to have a job and did not concern himself with the decisions being made by the National Park Service and the State Park Commission to bring the mission back to life.

ROBERT ZARAGOZA

I arrived and was assigned to Barracks E. The barracks leader was Gilbert Loya who showed me how to make the bed in military style and the stuff we had to do to keep the barracks clean. The group I arrived with were all from Los Angeles. My first job was on the adze crew with the beams for the buildings. Then they rotated us and then I worked on building the columns. And I put a lot of the tile on the roof. I did a lot of plastering, and whitewashing, too. We dug a lot of trenches between the buildings looking for artifacts. They just picked me for all this stuff. I didn't ask for it. They called me out on fire crews, too. I think I worked most places except for the woodshop.

They had all sizes of beams and some you could hardly move until they sawed them in the saw pit. All the crews were in competition with each other to see who could put out more work. They were very conscientious. They would argue about who could shovel faster. Visitors would come all the time to see the mission work, and one time they dressed me up like an Indian and took photographs. Getting into the CCC was one of the best things that ever happened to me. The Army only paid $21 a month and we were making $30.[18]

Zaragoza enrolled at age eighteen after hearing about the CCC from friends in his east Los Angeles neighborhood. Both his parents were Mexican immigrants and his father was a railroad worker. After processing at the CCC staging center in

Van Nuys, he was sent to La Purísima, where he liked it so much he re-enrolled twice. He was very adept at handcrafting and the foremen rotated him frequently to obtain the benefits of his high-quality work. He went home most weekends by train, or hitchhiked from Lompoc.[19]

> The truck drivers always picked us up. I remember after supper in camp they had classes to finish high school. That's what I should have done. I didn't know any better and only took a few vocational classes and played pool in the recreation hall. I used to watch the guys play poker, too.
>
> Everyone had a lot of respect for the barracks leaders. When we went to bed and they would say, "Lights out," we were supposed to be quiet. And everyone would be quiet and talk about it tomorrow. That's how much respect they had. Sometimes the older guys would sneak wine or beer into the barracks, and if they got caught, they had to clean the latrines on the weekend or peel potatoes in the kitchen.
>
> All the fellas used to call me Mr. Rules and Regulations because when they went to do something wrong, I would say, "You can't do that." They would say, "Why?" and I would say, "Because you're not supposed to." At night, they would say, "Let's go to the farm down the road and pick some fruit." And I would say, "You're not supposed to." So I was named Mr. Rules and Regulations.[20]

Black Enrollees

Among the earlier enrollees to work at the La Purísima reconstruction project were forty-five blacks from Los Angeles.[21] Supervisor Ed Negus had twenty on his crew at the Santa Rosa rock wall (an early project) and more at the mission site. He recalled they were good workers, but later they had to be transferred.

> In 1936 some enrollees from Virginia and West Virginia were brought in. They talked to the blacks at La Purísima the same way they talked to the blacks back home. But those boys from Los Angeles wouldn't take it from them. There were many fights and shortly afterward the blacks were separated out into their own camp at another location. A lot of them were really mad over that and a lot of them quit. It was too bad.[22]

CCC Camp Food

In camps across the country, the most important factor determining company morale was the food served to enrollees. The combination of nourishing food, hard work, and fresh air caused an average weight gain of ten pounds among new, usually undernourished, men. Some of the more isolated camps had to serve canned meats, canned vegetables, and canned milk more frequently, which created grumbling among the enrollees and letters from distressed mothers to Director Fechner in Washington. But most enrollees enjoyed the food served in the mess halls; some even called it the best food they had ever eaten.

The La Purísima Camp was fortunate to be located in the agriculturally rich Lompoc Valley, and the Army supply sergeants could easily acquire fresh meats, vegetables, and dairy products for the men. It boasted the biggest kitchen and mess hall in the Los Angeles CCC District with a capacity of 410 men for any meal.[23] In August, 1936, the camp enjoyed the ethnic food produced by a Chinese cook, Yee Look, whose chop suey received rave reviews in the CCC *News-Courier.*[24] Gilbert Ballesterose said he ate "like a king" at Camp Lisle, Camp Hawkins Bar, and at La Purísima.[25] He remembered all the baking was done in camp by nightshift enrollees apprenticing as bakers. Robert Zaragoza recalled how he gained weight with the La Purísima Camp's food.

> I put on about twenty pounds. I weighed 118 when I went in and 140 when I got out. I never ate so good in my life, to tell you the truth. And you got all you wanted. They made stew, steak, chicken, eggs in the morning, pie for dessert. Plenty of vegetables. The tables were set with big platters of food when we came in the mess hall. Whoever emptied the platter at the table had to go up to the kitchen counter and get it refilled from the cooks. Lots of new boys would come in with their eyes bigger than their stomachs and they would take more than they could eat. But they never had so much food before.[26]

Frank Hines remembered his days working in the kitchen.

> The food was good, well prepared, supervised by the camp doctor who came in to check the mess hall for cleanliness. We would have to let him inspect the food we were preparing. Captain Tornell would be the first one in each morning for his coffee out of the twenty-gallon urn. They used to contract with local markets and suppliers and they picked up fresh

ℰ MENU ℈

THURSDAY March 18, 1937

BREAKFAST

STEWED PRUNES
POSTS BRAN FLAKES
GOLDEN STATE GRADE A MILK
GRAPENUTS HOT CAKES
MAPLE SYRUP   BUTTER
CRULLERS
HOT COFFEE   CREAM   SUGAR

DINNER

MEXICAN CHILE BEANS
          HAMBURGER SAUCE
BOILED CARROTTS AND TURNIPS
LYONNAISE POTATOES
LETTUCE   SWEET VINEGAR SAUCE
BREAD   BUTTER
ICED TEA
RICE CUSTARD   SAUCE

SUPPER

VEGETABLE AND MACRONI SOUP
VIENNA MEAT LOAF
MEAT LOAF GRAVY
BUTTER MASHED POTATOES
BUTTERED STRING BEANS
COMBINATION COTTAGE CHEESE SALAD
BREAD   BUTTER
TRICOLATED COFFEE   CREAM   SUGAR
LEMON CREAM PIE

GEO W NELSON
Mess Steward

PAUL R BRAVENDER
1st Lt CA-Res 3rd CA(RAA)
Mess Officer

ALBERT H SATTERLEE
1st Lt Med-Res
Camp Surgeon

National Archives, Record Group 35, Washington, D.C.

[35]

Christmas, 1935

Menu

1951st Company, CCC
Purisima Camp SP=29
Lompoc, California

Lieut. K. N. Heyne
COMMANDING

Lieut. Claus A. Tornell
ADJUTANT

EDGAR L. McCRAE
E. E. P. INSTRUCTOR

LIEUT. EDGAR ROEHM
CAMP SURGEON

PETER R. QUIN
EDUCATIONAL ADVISOR.

Christmas menu (1935). [MISSION LA PURISIMA ARCHIVES]

A Merry Christmas
and a
Happy New Year

~ M E N U ~
CHRISTMAS DINNER
3 P.M.

STUFFED OLIVES   CRISP CELERY

OYSTER COCKTAIL   APPLE NUT SALAD

CLEAR CONSOMME

ROAST YOUNG TOM TURKEY
CHESTNUT DRESSING
GIBLET GRAVY

MASHED POTATOES   CANDIED SWEET POTATOES

BUTTERED BRUSSEL SPROUTS

CREAMED PEAS

PARKERHOUSE ROLLS

APPLE PIE   and   ICE CREAM

COFFEE

NUTS   FRUIT   CANDY   CIGARETTES

Christmas menu (1935). [MISSION LA PURISIMA ARCHIVES]

PERISHABLE FOOD PURCHASED

DATE July 10, 1940

PRECEDING
MONTH JUNE   SCS-9   P. O. LOMPOC   STATE CALIF.
CAMP NO. SP-29

Total Ra-tions	Smoked or Dried Meats	Beef Fresh	Lards	Pork Fresh	Cooked Meats	Veal Fresh	Frank-fur-ters	Hearts & Liver	Butter
7340	1182	2860	740	825	None	175	225	188	690

	Cheese	Poul-try	Eggs	Bread	Milk	Fish	Fresh Fruits	Vege-tables Fresh	Pota-toes
	75	482	750 doz.	4428	2580 qts.	275	$ 109.50	$ 239.34	6500

Amount of local purchases $ 398.34

Amount of Q. M. purchases $ 717.18

Amount purchased on contract $1929.81

Above items are to be recorded in the number of pounds.
Fresh fruits and fresh vegetables can be registered in cost.

Company strength beginning of month JUNE - 301

Any abnormal condition should be reported by Immediate Action Memorandum

(copies to be sent to Corps Area and District Commanders).

REMARKS:

National Archives, Record Group 35, Washington, D.C.

[38]

Well-oiled interior of Twin Camps Mess Hall (1938). [COURTESY OF GILBERT BALLESTEROSE]

produce and goods from the ice house in Lompoc. The food was excellent, and they always did something lavish for holidays—the men who stayed in camp at Thanksgiving and Christmas ate like kings. There was also a special shift of bakers working at night.

When the men first arrived in the mess hall, the food was already on the table. They would appoint one man from each table to come up to the serving counters and refill the table's platters and bowls. There was no problem getting seconds or thirds—they could have all they wanted. Their plates were all turned upside down when they first sat down at the table to keep the ever-present dust off them.[27]

Community Relations

The little agricultural town of Lompoc generally welcomed the CCC Camp members. Young local men did not appreciate competition for the young women of the community, causing occasional scuffles at the tavern on H Street, but most of the enrollees behaved themselves. Robert Zaragoza said, "The local boys didn't stand a chance because we outnumbered them."[28] If any parent came to camp to complain, "Please keep your boys away from our girls," the Army commander's stock reply was, "Please keep your girls away from our boys."[29]

Dating of local girls was rare because they had been told by their parents to be wary of the CCC boys. Even handsome young men like Frank Hines found that "It was awfully hard to get acquainted with them."[30] Most of the men had girlfriends back home. Enrollees were forbidden to have their own automobiles, but some at La Purísima had cars which they kept hidden in wooded areas near the camp so they could drive home on weekends.[31] Since most of the enrollees were from a much larger city, they chose not to bother with Lompoc and went home to Los Angeles on weekends. Those who did walk the two miles into town from the mission site usually went to drink liquor which was forbidden in camp, or to see a movie, or to go to a high school basketball game, or to church. Most of the men were too young to purchase liquor, so they chose the oldest-looking man to purchase a bottle which they would share.[32]

Ray Ellis described walking into Lompoc in the evening.

> We went in to town to see a movie about once every week or two, and there was a big apple orchard on the right hand side of the road. We would arrive in town with a few apples in our pockets. They were such good apples! Yellow Delicious. Coming back to camp, there was a field of watermelons that the guys used to steal, too. This particular night, we took a watermelon and the farmer shot at us with buckshot. He didn't hit us, but it scared the devil out of us. I kept the watermelon and ran with it. The farmer came and complained to the company commander, but they never caught us.[33]

Gilbert Ballesterose knew of another incident with a local farmer.

> There was a farm beside the mission site and they had a pig there that was always breaking loose. He would get out all the time and I used to see him when I was driving on the road. He was an old pig and we avoided him. I tried not to hit him with my truck, and the company commander complained to the farmer who owned this pig since it was becoming a safety hazard. The farmer was disgusted and said, "You can have him." So the camp got a pig, and the guys built a corral for it. The cook gave him all the slop and he grew big. They butchered him one Fourth of July when he got too big to take care of and they had a big feast.[34]

Ed Negus

While waiting for the mission excavations to be completed and the plans and specifications prepared, the Santa Rosa Company occupied the time by clearing the river bottom of the Santa Ynez River from the town of Surf on the Pacific coast eastward almost to Buellton. They also cleared and arranged two sites for public parks, one at Nojoqui Falls Park near Solvang, and the other at Santa Rosa Park, about thirteen miles east of Lompoc.[35]

National Park Service Construction Foreman Edward Negus described the work at Santa Rosa Park.

> During the first year, while the state acquired the property for the mission, the CCC camp worked on the fifteen-foot-high rock wall at Santa Rosa Park. They wanted to build a parking lot and a stone wall. I knew a little bit about concrete, but I'm not a stonemason. It was quite an undertaking to go out there with forty to sixty boys because we had to carry rocks around to where we needed them. To get big rocks strong enough to hold up a wall, you can't be using rocks you can carry in your hands. A lot of the rocks were 100 to 200 pounds and we had to manhandle them to get them down there to start building that wall.[36]

Negus's Employment Interview

Negus described why he was hired for the mission project. At only twenty-six years old, he was the youngest foreman working for the NPS at the time.[37]

> The CCC Camp was built where the mission's garden is today, and it was just a tent city to start with. When I arrived, Harvey Johnson was the National Park Service project superintendent, and he was holding a vacancy open for me. Hageman, the architect, interviewed me about how much time it would take to build the Santa Rosa Park rock wall and how much rock a man could lay in one day. I told him that it could be easy depending on how big the rocks were and what shape they were in and how much they had to be cut and chiseled to fit. If the rocks were heavy, a man would have a hell of a time.
>
> The wall they wanted to build out there was about 1,500 cubic yards of rocks, and I asked where were they going to get all those rocks. Hageman said they would get them along the county roads. I told him, "Do you

know how much that is, 1,500 cubic yards of rocks? That's forty railroad car loads of rocks! There aren't that many rocks along the roads anywhere around here." I knew that a railroad car holds about forty cubic yards of rock. Harvey Johnson was a retired railroad engineer and he told me later that when I knew how much rock it was, he and Hageman knew they were talking to the right man for the job.

Hageman handed me a roll of drawings and said, "Here, this is your job." He described what it was going to look like according to some old drawings and paintings he had. He asked me what I thought of it and if I could visualize it. All I could see was a helluva lot of work if that was what they wanted.

They did pick up a lot of rocks from along the road, but got most of them from a sandstone formation on a hillside near where the parking lot was going to be. I didn't know anything about dynamiting so they got a county employee to come out and be in charge of the powder. He trained one of the CCC boys in how to do it and the boy took charge and handled the powder. They blasted the sandstone loose and backed up the dump truck into it and rolled the rocks over into the dump truck. The dump truck dumped them near where the wall was going to be, then we had to manhandle them and roll them and handbar them.

A handbar is like a wheelbarrow with a man on the front and back, like a stretcher, and you carry the rock between you. Lots of times, the rock was so heavy, it took four men on each corner. We were out there all fall of 1934 and getting pretty good headway on it when winter came. The rain and cold made the north slope of the hill too slippery to work so they sent us out to Nojoqui Park to build trails, bridges, and barbecue pits. When the weather got dry again, we got back on the Santa Rosa rock wall. Then they called me to come in and work on the mission.[38]

1. Civilian Conservation Corps, Los Angeles District, *Official Annual,* Ninth Corps Area (Van Nuys, California, 1938), p. 76.
2. *Lompoc Record,* August 10, 1934.
3. La Purísima Advisory Committee *Minutes,* August 8, 1934, Mission La Purísima Archives, Lompoc, California.
4. Santa Barbara County *Resolution* No. 1421, September 24, 1934, correspondence files, Mission La Purísima Archives, Lompoc, California.
5. CCC *Annual,* p. 76.
6. Ibid.

7. Lawrence C. Merriam letter to H.V. Johnson, August 22, 1934, correspondence files, Mission La Purísima Archives, Lompoc, California.
8. CCC *Annual,* p. 77.
9. "La Purísima CCC Camp Inspection Reports, 1934-1941," Box 37, Record Group 35, National Archives and Records Service, General Services Administration (Washington, D.C.).
10. M. Gilbert Ballesterose Interview with Christine E. Savage, Buellton, California, July 26, 1989.
11. Ibid.
12. Ibid.
13. Ibid.
14. Franklin E. Hines Interview with Christine E. Savage, Los Angeles, California, July 21, 1989.
15. Ibid.
16. Ibid.
17. Ibid.
18. Robert Zaragosa Interview with Christine E. Savage, Los Angeles, California, July 24, 1989.
19. Ibid.
20. Ibid.
21. Edward Negus Interview with Christine E. Savage, Lompoc, California, July 19, 1989.
22. Ibid.
23. Civilian Conservation Corps, Los Angeles District, *News-Courier,* semi-monthly newspaper, Van Nuys, California, April 15, 1937.
24. *News-Courier,* August 1, 1936.
25. Ballesterose Interview.
26. Zaragoza Interview.
27. Hines Interview.
28. Zaragoza Interview.
29. Hines Interview.
30. Ibid.
31. Ballesterose Interview; Ellis Interview.
32. Hines Interview.
33. Raymond E. Ellis, Sr., interview with Christine E. Savage, Santa Barbara, California, July 27, 1989.
34. Ballesterose Interview.
35. CCC *Annual,* p. 77.
36. Negus Interview.
37. Ibid.
38. Ibid.

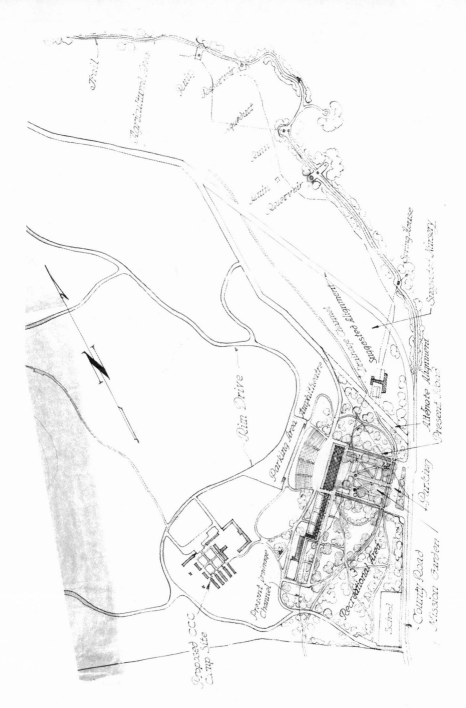

Early reconstruction drawing for mission complex. It was never implemented. Note amphitheater behind padres' residence building. [MISSION LA PURISIMA ARCHIVES]

4. Project Management

Advisory Committee Established

La Purísima's chief architect, Frederick C. Hageman, described the next critical steps in La Purísima's reconstruction.

> In order to plan the work intelligently, it was necessary to formulate a definite policy of restoration with a fixed objective. The State Park Commission asked a group of seven Santa Barbara County residents to form the La Purísima Advisory Committee. They made a thorough study of the possibilities, and on September 24, 1935, released a comprehensive report which outlined restoration policy. The report was accepted by the state and National Park Service authorities without change, and was used as a guide in setting up the master plan for the mission site.
>
> The policy, which was conscientiously adhered to throughout the restoration program, was to make every effort to authenticate features of architectural design and construction by documentary or photographic evidence, or by evidence established from study of the ruined buildings themselves, or by first-hand information collected from early settlers of the region, and from study of original structures still existing at other California missions. Adherence to this policy provided assurance that the finished structures would be faithful reproductions of the original buildings, and that a minimum of design and construction would be left to conjecture.[1]

In January 1935 the first members of the La Purísima Advisory Committee were:
—Wallace C. Penfield, engineer and secretary of Santa Barbara County Planning Commission;
—Pearl Chase, chair of the Plans and Planting Committee of the Community Arts Association of Santa Barbara and chair of the Santa Barbara County Roadside Committee;

[45]

—Dr. Frederic E. Clements, director of the Santa Barbara Ecological Research Station for the Carnegie Institution of Washington and consultant to the National Park Service;

—C. Kelley Hardenbrook, deputy district attorney for Santa Barbara County, Lompoc District;

—Marion Parks, historian for the Santa Barbara Parlor of the Native Daughters of the Golden West;

—L. Deming Tilton, director of the State Planning Commission and director of the Santa Barbara County Planning Commission;

—Carleton Monroe Winslow, vice chair of State Historic Buildings Committee and prominent Spanish Colonial architect in Santa Barbara and Los Angeles.

Ex-officio Advisory Committee members were:

—Ronald M. Adam, Santa Barbara County supervisor, Lompoc District, and editor of the *Lompoc Record*;

—Frank Dunne, Santa Barbara County forester and County Park superintendent;

—H.W. Whitsitt, National Park Service architect and project superintendent of La Purísima CCC Camp;

—Frederick C. Hageman, National Park Service staff architect for La Purísima reconstruction project.[2]

Other people later included as Advisory Committee members were:

—Dr. William H. Ellison, History Department, Santa Barbara State College; .
—Fr. Patrick Roddy, O.F.M., of the Santa Barbara Mission;
—Harvey Johnson, former project superintendent of Santa Rosa CCC Camp;
—H.V. Smith, subsequent project superintendent of La Purísima CCC Camp.[3]

The Construction Foremen

Foreman Ed Negus was born and raised in Lompoc, and as a child had even played among the ruins of the first Mission La Purísima at the present day cul-de-sac of F Street below Locust. He grew up in a construction contracting family, went to work for his father's business after high school, and was acting as foreman at job sites within three or four years because he had become an expert in both carpentry and handling concrete.[4]

When the Depression hit in 1929, Miguelito Park in Lompoc wanted a dance floor builder. They got me to go up there in charge of welfare labor and build the dance floor. When they built the new county parks under WPA work, I couldn't get on there because my dad was a carpenter on the same job, and no two members of one family could be on the same project. So the county put me on as a laborer so I could pour concrete floors and finish them. I became well acquainted with the Santa Barbara County supervisors and officials from handling concrete. When they were ready to build the La Purísima CCC Camp, they told me to come out because they had a job for me. I was busy and didn't come, and they called me for two weeks. Then one day Walt Stewart came and told me if I didn't get out there right away, I would lose a good job.[5]

Walter E. Stewart was another construction foreman at La Purísima and spent most of his time on carpentry. He was in charge of producing all the doors, shutters, ballustrades, benches, and other furniture. He, too, was a construction contractor in Lompoc, and he sometimes competed against Negus's father for business, and sometimes worked with him.[6] Both Stewart and Negus were what the CCC administration in Washington called Local Experienced Men, or LEMs. The LEMs, most of whom were veterans of World War I, were hired at each CCC worksite across the country. They managed and trained the crews of enrollees under the supervision of government agents who were usually from the Forest Service or the National Park Service.

Walt Stewart and Ronald Adam, Santa Barbara County supervisor (and ex-officio member of the La Purísima Advisory Committee), were close friends, and worked out an arrangement to borrow lumber for La Purísima's scaffolding from Santa Barbara County's stock. When the mission site needed lumber, the County put in an extra large order for bridge timbers and some of these ended up in the mission's scaffolding.[7] Both Stewart and Adam kept pestering Negus to come to work at La Purísima.

Camp Hierarchy

The Civilian Conservation Corps had a complex chain of command from President Roosevelt, through Director Fechner, on to the various governmental agencies managing the camps. Each camp also had its own hierarchy with Army officers, Technical Services personnel from government agencies, and the LEMs all governing the work site and camp life. As the La Purísima project was getting off the ground, the chain of command was still being decided, presenting a problem for Ed Negus.

EMERGENCY CONSERVATION WORK CAMPS

DATE ...June 17, 1938........

CAMP No. SP-29..................

STATE OF .California.........

TECHNICAL PERSONNEL

Fill in on this sheet, name of technical supervisors, not enrolled men, and amount of salary they receive.

NAME	OCCUPATION	SALARY
SMITH, Howard V.	Proj. Supt.	2300PA
ROWE, Edwin D.	Landscape Foreman	2040PA
HAGEMAN, Frederick C.	Sr. Foreman (Arch)	2000PA
HARWOOD, Harvey R.	Sr. Foreman (Arch)	2000PA
AMES, Ralph E.	Foreman (Const.)	1860PA
NEGUS, Edward	Foreman (Const.)	1860PA
STEWART, Walter A.	Foreman (Const.)	1800PA
CASSUTH, William H.	Mechanic	125PM
JOLLY, Wiley E.	Jr. Asst. to Tech.	1020PA
THOMPSON, John Q.	Mechanic's Helper	70PM
GIL, Lawrence J.	Blacksmith's Helper	70PM
LOYA, Gilbert M.	Tool Sharpener's Helper	70PM

La Purísima project foremen and LEMs (1938). [NATIONAL ARCHIVES, RECORD GROUP 35, WASHINGTON, D.C.]

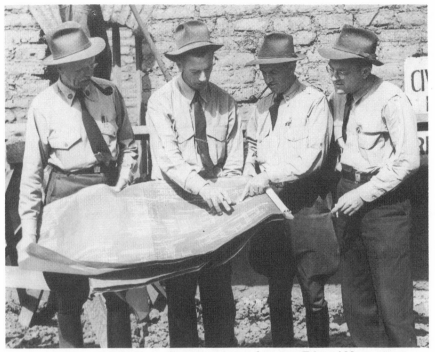

LEFT TO RIGHT: Edwin Denys Rowe, landscape foreman; Edward Negus, construction foreman; H.V. "Vee" Smith, project superintendent; Frederick C. Hageman, architect (1938). [MISSION LA PURISIMA ARCHIVES]

On the Santa Rosa rock wall I was hired as a foreman, but I was signed up as a junior foreman when they brought me in to the mission site. I had the biggest work crews to supervise, but there were some situations when the other foremen thought I should be watching their crews, too. One time [Landscape Foreman] Ed Rowe bawled me out for not watching his crew, and one time [NPS Civil Engineer] Art Darsey gave me the devil for not saving his survey station [ground stakes marking wall alignment]. He chewed me out good for that. Walt Stewart chewed me out one day when I was having trouble with the trucks, so when I finished work that day I told Harvey Johnson to take the damn job and shove it.

Every evening after work when we came back to camp, the kids had to be returned to the Army at 4:00 in the afternoon, and from 4:00 to 5:00 all six foremen met in the NPS office so any requests for materials or trucks could be planned. Things would be discussed here and that's when I blew up. I didn't care at that point and I went home.

[49]

Harvey Johnson called me up the next morning and told me to come back to work. I told him I quit because of everybody giving me hell and blaming me for everything, and I was handling the biggest part of the crew. Johnson said, "I am sorry you were signed up as a junior foreman. You should be a foreman like the rest of them." He said to come back to work and that night there would be a meeting in the office. When I came in that night with the crew, Johnson told the foremen that no one could give orders except the project superintendent and from then on, if they wanted anything, they had to ask him. He was looking right at Darsey as much as anybody else when he said it. So when they moved the camp up on the hill and started calling it La Purísima Camp, I was promoted to construction foreman and fire suppression foreman. So it was official.[8]

Handling the Crews

Negus described his first days as construction foreman at the mission site.

I had not studied up on the mission in any way, shape or form. My job was to direct and teach the kids. Harvey Johnson had told me when I was supervising at the Santa Rosa Park rock wall, "Don't try to make these boys work, teach them to work." To me that meant a helluva lot, and I took the meaning don't stand back and holler do this and do that, but get right in and teach them. Show them what you want. Hageman was very much the same way.

If the boys took an interest in their work, you gave them a chance with a little of this and some of that. You didn't keep them in the mudpit all the time. As soon as you get a couple of kids going on something, you move a couple of more kids in to help them. And then you've got four or five kids working on that. Then you gradually moved other kids around as much as you could.

For some reason, the outstanding kids seemed to want to be laying brick. It was a lot better than mixing mud or running bricks on the wheelbarrow. Each brick weighed sixty-five pounds and you could only put two bricks at a time on a wheelbarrow. The first couple of years on the mission project, we didn't have rubber tires on the wheelbarrows, just old iron tires. If you hit a little rock with an iron tire, it didn't bounce over and the bricks inside would crack. Even then, we needed an iron hook with a rope to pull the wheelbarrows up to the top of a sixteen-foot-high wall. They needed help going up there.

When they brought me in from the Santa Rosa rock wall, they had already started some of the adobe work on the north end of the residence building. That first year, another foreman, Win Keerl, was developing the adobe brick-making process. The whole area in front of the mission was smoothed off to make a place to mold the adobe bricks. They had already started on the upper end of the building and they had laid out where the columns were going to be and the doorways, and so forth.

I had a crew of forty to fifty kids working with everybody doing something. To see that they are doing it the way you want it done and all these various things, I had to be back and forth. Some were laying bricks, some were tying up the steel reinforcing rods, some building scaffolding, putting up ceiling joists, pouring concrete, and cleaning up. I was all over all the time. I walked my legs off![9]

Teaching the CCC men how to work was Negus's biggest challenge. He worked right beside them, showing them what to do, and he felt that made a big difference in the way he got along with "the kids" throughout the project. "I never asked them to do any work I wouldn't do right beside them," he said.[10] If an enrollee didn't apply himself to the job, Negus would ask that boy to "help" him personally. After a few hours, the reluctant worker usually performed better on his own to avoid being asked to "help" Negus again. When the members of a crew were all getting along well, Negus liked to let them decide for themselves who would be best at specific assignments.

One day at the Santa Rosa rock wall, Negus had to cope with a difficult crew.

There were no bulldozers at La Purísima in 1934, so earth moving was pick-and-shovel work. Fifty boys were transferred from the Los Prietos CCC Camp and Harvey Johnson told me they had caused problems at their previous work sites. I took twenty-five of them out to the rock wall and worked with them. The assistant leader on the crew, Barney Hughes, had one new boy who refused to work. Barney was an LEM who was a veteran of World War I, about forty, and was a former lightweight boxing champ. The new boy spoke sharply to Barney who ordered him back to work. The new boy took a swing at Barney, but Barney knocked him down with two punches. I stopped the fight and told everyone to go back to work, and made the boy with the bloody nose work alongside me.

After work was over that day and we were back in camp, I described the incident to Lieutenant Nesen, Captain Clinton's assistant. The new boy had been cussing Barney out and Barney only knocked him down after the kid took the first swing. The kid asked for it and I defended Barney as the assistant leader of the crew. Lt. Nesen described the incident to the assembled camp at retreat that night before supper, and the new boy wouldn't talk to me for a long time. He had a husky friend, Tex, who also didn't like me because of that day on the rock wall. But Tex was a fine worker and I eventually rated him as a Crew Leader.[11]

Negus had strong memories of the conscientiousness of enrollees.

The kids teamed up together and would ask, "Can I work with so-and-so?" or "I can't get along with this guy." So the kids that wanted to work together were more interested in what they were doing. The kids took pride in their work. Practically all the boys were from Los Angeles and the work was so different from anything they had ever been around before. I always had a job ready for newcomers—something they would be very busy at—and I'd stay pretty close to that bunch for two or three days and work with them. When they saw all the other kids working, there was usually not much argument about it.

One boy sprained his ankle at another CCC camp and complained that it hurt each time he worked. They kept him in quarters [the camp infirmary] as long as they could, but they finally told him he would have to go to work or be discharged. He wanted a medical discharge. I put him to work on the chapel in the residence building grinding the edges of adobe bricks to fit into the arches over the doorways. It was a dirty job because of the grinding dust, but he could sit down to do it. He complained after a while that he was tired of grinding bricks, so I moved him to clean-up duty at the bottom of the walls, and some wheelbarrow work. Finally, he told his co-workers to go jump in the lake and refused to work. He said, "I won't do this for you or anybody else."

I took him to the Army office when I heard that, because what they were waiting for was a refusal to work. They gave him a discharge, but in one month an investigator came from Washington, D.C., to examine the incident. I described how the boy was given different assignments when his ankle hurt and how he finally refused to work. The investigator never returned, but we were surprised that the boy had enough pull to have the situation looked into.

That was the only time I remember that a boy refused to work. Almost all of them were very conscientious because they were interested in their work. They had safety instruction once a week. The Army ration for each man was forty-six cents a day, plus clothing, shelter, and transportation. The NPS paid the salaries of the supervisors, so it cost the government about $6.00 a day for each CCC worker who was paid $1.00 a day. At that time, a man could get a pretty good job for $4 or $5 a day, so they valued the care provided by the government.[12]

1. Frederick C. Hageman and Olaf T. Hagen, *Mission La Purísima Concepción—A Glance Through its History and the Story of its Restoration,* National Park Service, United States Department of the Interior (undated), Mission La Purísima Archives, Lompoc, California, p. 15.
2. La Purísima Advisory Committee *Minutes,* March 27, 1936, Mission La Purísima Archives, Lompoc, California.
3. La Purísima Advisory Committee *Minutes,* November 10, 1936, Mission La Purísima Archives, Lompoc, California.
4. Edward Negus interview with Christine E. Savage, Lompoc, California, July 19, 1989.
5. Ibid.
6. Ibid.
7. Ibid.
8. Ibid.
9. Ibid.
10. Ibid.
11. Ibid.
12. Ibid.

5. Preserve or Rebuild?

Hageman's Research

The State Park Commission took a piecemeal approach to approval of the La Purísima project; by March 1935, they had only approved the reconstruction of the padres' Residence Building among the mission complex of thirteen buildings.[1] Despite this official irresolution, it quickly became evident that an enormous amount of painstaking research work would have to be done, for little historic data on the mission's architecture was available. Fortunately, the task of conducting this research was assumed by Fred Hageman when the Advisory Committee recommended his appointment as supervising architect in May 1935.[2] A driven man, Hageman was only twenty-eight when he began working at La Purísima in 1934, yet he was the energetic force behind the authenticity of the reconstruction project. It was his thorough consideration with historical and archaeological evidence that made the restoration project such a success.

Hageman searched out original records and documents of Mission La Purísima, correspondence of the padres, and private photographic collections. He interviewed early settlers about the mission, and visited other missions to study their features. He also made use of architectural drawings of other California missions provided by the Historic American Buildings Survey, another New Deal Program begun in November 1933.[3] Ed Negus watched Hageman use Southern Pacific Railroad photos from the 1890s to calculate the former locations of doors and windows in the mission ruins, from the point of view of the photographer.[4]

Architect's Background

Hageman was born in Los Angeles, and attended Los Angeles High School and the University of Southern California, from which he later received a Bachelor of Science degree in architectural engineering in 1928.[5] Ed Negus described one of Hageman's early architectural influences.

OFFICE OF THE
PRESIDENT AND PUBLISHER

November 13, 1935.

Mr. Fred C. Hageman,
La Purisima Camp, S.P.-29,
Lompoc, California.

Dear Mr. Hageman:

On returning to Oakland I located some negatives
which I took of La Purisima Mission in 1904. These may
be of interest to you. I am sending these, together with
some other photographs which may prove even of greater
interest, and which were taken in 1875. Two of them are of
the interior of Purisima Mission, and one is taken on the
side of the mission opposite the pepper tree. I am not
positive as to who took those photographs, although it may
have been Tabor in San Francisco, or another old photographer
of the early days from whom I obtained quite a number of old
mission pictures.

In looking up my references to Purisima, I notice
that there is a story about Purisima Mission restoration which
appeared in the Out West Magazine, volume 23, pages 256 to 264.
I have the bound volumes of Out West only up to that year,
but I am sending to the State Library to have the article
copied for me.

Permit me to reiterate that I was very much pleased
with the work, and do not believe that there is anything that
could possibly be criticised.

Very sincerely yours,

J. R. Knowland

The signature on this letter is that of Joseph W. Knowland, chair of the State Park
Commission, president and publisher of the *Oakland Tribune,* state senator, chair of
the Historic Landmarks Committee of the Native Sons of the Golden West, and
founding president of the California Historical Landmarks League. [MISSION LA
PURISIMA ARCHIVES]

4-35-10M

S-1710

Southern Pacific Company

65 MARKET STREET, SAN FRANCISCO, CALIFORNIA

IN REPLY PLEASE REFER TO

F. S. McGINNIS,
VICE-PRESIDENT
SYSTEM PASSENGER TRAFFIC
F. S. HOWARD,
ASSISTANT TO VICE-PRESIDENT
F. E. WATSON,
ASSISTANT TO VICE-PRESIDENT
F. Q. TREDWAY,
GENERAL ADVERTISING MANAGER

September 20, 1935   KD-

Mr. H. W. Whitsitt,
Superintendent, Santa Rosa Park Camp SP-29,
Lompoc, California

Dear Mr. Whitsitt:

Thank you for your letter September 10th requesting photographs of the La Purisma Mission near Lompoc, California, to assist your camp in its efforts to reconstruct this Mission as accurately as possible.

We are happy to advise you that we have secured a print of the particular photograph you mention in your letter, and that we have also secured 15 other photographs of the Mission, which we are sending you herewith.   These photographs were taken by Mr. H. C. Tibbitts, San Francisco photographer, in the years 1906 and 1913.

We have checked with the State Chamber of Commerce and they advise that the McCurry Photo Service of Sacramento have in their files photographs of the La Purisma Mission taken around the year 1880, and that no doubt you can secure prints by writing to them.

The project of restoring this Mission will help to preserve another link in the colorful history of the State, and you and your camp are to be congratulated for undertaking this commendable work, and we appreciate your having given us the opportunity to be of some assistance.

Yours very truly,

F S McGinnis

LEADING TRAINS ON SOUTHERN PACIFIC'S
FOUR GREAT ROUTES

"SUNSET LIMITED" SAN FRANCISCO-LOS ANGELES-NEW ORLEANS   "SAN FRANCISCO OVERLAND LIMITED" SAN FRANCISCO-CHICAGO
"GOLDEN STATE LIMITED" LOS ANGELES-CHICAGO   "CASCADE" SAN FRANCISCO-PORTLAND-SEATTLE

[MISSION LA PURISIMA ARCHIVES]

After his sophomore year, he and another student got a job on a boat and went to Europe. He always wanted to study architecture in Paris, so they got a couple of bicycles and went to Paris. He was very fascinated with stairways and balconies and so on in Paris, and created a large sketchbook of different balconies and twisted and odd-shaped stairways. He showed me that sketchbook a couple of times.

When the three-month summer vacation was up, the other boy came back to America to return to school, but Hageman wasn't satisfied yet and wanted to see more. He spent almost a year in Paris; then, when he was ready to come home, he couldn't get a ticket because he had jumped ship. He didn't have a visa, passport, anything, and it took him quite a while to finally get permission to come back.[6]

Architect Frederick C. Hageman walking before the newly restored padres' resident building (April 1937). [MISSION LA PURISIMA ARCHIVES]

Hageman then attended the University of California at Los Angeles for one year, studying advanced architectural design and earning membership in scholarly and professional architectural fraternities. After college, he apprenticed with a Los Angeles architect, A.B. Sturges, to earn the two years' work experience the State of California required before he could take his state exam and become licensed.[7] But Hageman left his apprenticeship before his two years were completed, and became an orchard and ranch supervisor with extra work in real estate management.

Hageman arrived in Santa Barbara in 1929 and affiliated with the noted architects Edwards and Plunkett. It was here that he became chief draftsman and acquired valuable experience as a designer and specification writer. He also helped design the interior of the Fox-Arlington Theater.[8] Negus elaborated on Hageman's involvement with this Santa Barbara landmark.

> Before the architect could get the plans completely finished, they let the contractor in there to build. Enough of the plans were drawn to get a building permit, but the finishing touches and actual design of it, Hageman had to do after they had already started construction on it. If you have ever been in the Fox-Arlington Theater, notice the seats along the side and the balconies along the stairs. He was real proud of that.[9]

Hageman freelanced for some time until the Depression began to affect the number of jobs available in Santa Barbara. He then took positions in the local administrative offices of the Civil Works Administration (CWA) and the State Emergency Relief Administration (SERA).[10]

Santa Barbara County Planning Commission Engineer Wallace Penfield got to know Hageman during this time, and when the county acquired title to the Mission La Purísima site from Union Oil, Penfield would consider only Hageman for the job of architect at the preservation project. When he came to the Santa Rosa Camp in August 1934, Hageman was hired as a senior foreman—not as project superintendent—by the National Park Service because he still did not have his state architectural license.[11] He made all the reconstruction drawings and plans for the Santa Rosa Park project, and it took the CCC men fifteen months to build what Hageman had drawn.[12]

When he turned his attention to the mission reconstruction project, Hageman brought his European studies as well as his American architectural training to the job. By the summer of 1935, he had acquired a personal appreciation for building with adobe, and wrote "Wally" Penfield, "I am becoming more and more impressed with this adobe construction. I'd sure like to build myself a house of it."[13]

[58]

Hageman was finally promoted to project superintendent at La Purísima on December 3, 1935,[14] although he did not become state certified and listed in the California Directory of Architects until 1940.[15]

Throughout the project, Ed Negus worked closely with Hageman to interpret his designs.

> Hageman was a good-natured fellow, but very explicit as to what he wanted and very exact in his drawings. He had thirty or forty boys at the mission excavating around the old ruins, getting data on where the doors were and other information so he could produce the drawings. He was a damn good teacher, and taught me a lot about reinforcing and fabricating steel.[16]

The Preserve or Rebuild Dilemma

Hageman wrote of the essential predicament in any historic preservation project.

> The excavation of the ruined buildings involved a major problem. It was uncertain just how stable the old walls would be once the mounds of eroded earth were removed. After excavation was completed, the Advisory Committee made the decision to preserve the walls and incorporate them in the new construction. Many problems developed as a result of the adoption of this policy, which had to be solved by trial and error.
>
> Had the old walls been torn down and cleared away, and construction started entirely new from the foundations, the size and appearance of the individual adobe bricks, floor tiles, and other structural elements would have had to be only relatively exact as there would have been no basis for comparison. But since the new and the old had to be fitted in together without any apparent break, it was very essential that reproduction of the original elements should be as exact as possible. This involved consideration not only of types, amounts, and sources of supply of the different materials, but shapes of the molds and changes in size [of the bricks] due to shrinkage during the process of drying or burning.[17]

On July 7, 1937, UC Berkeley historian Dr. Herbert E. Bolton, a member of the National Park Service Advisory Board, declared that the educational value of the mission site would be lost if the remaining ruins were to be only stabilized and studied. After a survey of the site, he advocated to the National Park Service a complete reconstruction of all known buildings at the La Purísima site.[18]

Professional Consultants

The National Park Service provided two consultants to the La Purísima Advisory Committee for the reconstruction project: Dr. Mark R. Harrington, curator of the Southwest Museum in Los Angeles, and Dr. Arthur A. Woodward, director of history and anthropology at the Los Angeles County Museum.[19] They both wrote reports advocating a complete reconstruction of the mission ruins for their value as educational structures. Both contended that mere preserved partial walls were less valuable educationally.

All of Hageman's architectural designs and supporting data were reviewed by the regional historian and technicians at the San Francisco Regional Office of the National Park Service, and by more historians at the Washington, D.C., office to ensure authenticity in his plans.[20] All the historical consulting and double-checking paid off in the form of a coherent policy resolution rendered a little over a year after La Purísima's CCC camp was established.

Advisory Committee's Recommendations

On September 24, 1935, the La Purísima Advisory Committee had presented its preliminary report to the State Park Commission. The report stressed the educational aspects of the site with "the preservation of the atmosphere of an authentic mission community in its natural setting."[21] They proposed that the National Park Service reconstruct every building that could be reproduced authentically from the evidence available. In the depths of the Depression, seven residents of Santa Barbara County told the federal government how to spend its money on a California state historic landmark.

At its meeting on November 14, 1936, the State Park Commission unanimously backed the Advisory Committee's recommendation that all known mission buildings be restored,[22] and continued to grant reconstruction approvals until building plans ceased to be made at the onset of World War II. On September 20, 1938, the Commission authorized the complete restoration of the three largest buildings in the mission complex, along with period furniture, and a partial restoration of the mission's water system.[23] On March 4, 1939, the Commission authorized the reconstruction of three Christianized Chumash dwellings,[24] and in

March 1941, allocated $10,000 to acquire more land for the La Purísima State Park site.

All these decisions and allocations were still years in the future after the debris was first cleared from the mission walls.

---

1. William E. Colby letter to Colonel Charles B. Wing, October 11, 1935, correspondence files, Mission La Purísima Archives, Lompoc, California.
2. La Purísima Advisory Committee *Minutes,* May 8, 1935, Mission La Purísima Archives, Lompoc, California.
3. Frederick C. Hageman and Olaf T. Hagen, *Mission La Purísima Concepción—A Glance Through its History and the Story of its Restoration,* National Park Service, United States Department of the Interior (undated), Mission La Purísima Archives, Lompoc, California, p. 16.
4. Edward Negus Interview with Christine E. Savage, Lompoc, California, July 19, 1989.
5. Russell Holmes Fletcher, ed., *Who's Who in California, 1942-43,* Vol. 1, Who's Who Publications (Los Angeles, 1943), p. 367; *Voice of the Twin Camps,* La Purísima CCC Camp, Lompoc, California, December 6, 1935.
6. Negus Interview.
7. Fletcher, op. cit.
8. Ibid.
9. Negus Interview.
10. *Voice,* December 6, 1935.
11. Ibid.
12. Negus Interview.
13. Frederick C. Hageman letter to Wallace C. Penfield, July 28, 1935, correspondence files, Mission La Purísima Archives, Lompoc, California.
14. *Voice,* December 6, 1935.
15. Certificate No. 350 issued 1940. *Directory of Certified Architects,* California State Board of Architectural Examiners (Sacramento, 1966), p. 110.
16. Negus Interview.
17. Hageman and Hagen, op. cit., pp. 17-18.
18. Herbert E. Bolton letter to Arthur E. Demaray, July 1, 1937, correspondence files, Mission La Purísima Archives, Lompoc, California.
19. Hageman and Hagen, op. cit., p. 16.
20. Ibid.
21. La Purísima Advisory Committee, *Report,* September 24, 1935, correspondence files, Mission La Purísima Archives, Lompoc, California, p. 1.
22. California State Park Commission *Minutes,* November 14, 1936, correspondence files, Mission La Purísima Archives, Lompoc, California.
23. State Park Commission *Minutes,* September 20, 1938, correspondence files, Mission La Purísima Archives, Lompoc, California.
24. State Park Commission *Minutes,* March 4, 1939, correspondence files, Mission La Purísima Archives, Lompoc, California.

6. From the Ground Up

Excavation of Ruins

In November 1934, the entire State Park Commission visited La Purísima to inspect the ruins and the excavation work.[1] Hageman and Johnson gave them a tour of the project, and Hageman described the excavation procedures in one of his many reports to the Commission, the National Park Service, and the La Purísima Advisory Committee.

> Crews of CCC enrollees, under supervision of the NPS technical staff were engaged in removal of thousands of yards of soil which had been

Four enrollees working inside residence building ruin removing debris. Original adobe walls in background. View looking north (February 1935). [MISSION LA PURISIMA ARCHIVES]

deposited on the site by the strong prevailing winds. In some locations the soil reached a depth of eight feet. In clearing away the debris around the ruined buildings, the eroded adobe earth from the old walls was carefully saved and later recast into new bricks. Diligent watch was kept for any artifacts that might be unearthed and many were found which furnished valuable information. The ruins of thirteen buildings were located, including a neophyte barracks 554 feet long, in addition to the extensive water system of tile pipelines, aqueducts, and fountains.[2]

Under the direction of the foremen, enrollees kept field notebooks while the excavation and reconstruction were being conducted. Selections from enrollee Guy F. Warren's *Field Notebook No. 3* read like a diary of the work progress, complete with drawings.

> January 7, 1935—Cut grass adjacent to mission walls. Started to excavate for corners of structure. Found corridor floors on east side paved with tile, $10\frac{1}{4} \times 10\frac{1}{4} \times 2$. Also in corridor in front of east door of chapel found small pieces of glazed terra cotta. Seventeen men in crew.
>
> January 14, 1935—No work on account of rain.
>
> January 17, 1935—Continued excavating of foundations of mission. Began clearing and leveling of ground for making of adobe bricks. Thirty-six men on job.
>
> January 24, 1935—Excavating on mission walls and foundations. Twenty-nine men on job. Finished on excavation of open water carrier's connection to reservoir No. 7 and prepared it for photographing. Removed stump from south end of east wall of mission. Two men cutting stakes.[3]

The Field Notebook continues into May, when the crews began to catch numerous gophers in traps each day. Warren ended his notebook by writing that the mud pits for adobe mortar mixing were begun on June 3, 1935.

From the inception of Company 1951 until May 1935, Harvey Johnson was NPS project superintendent of the mission reconstruction work.[4] An elderly man, Johnson didn't see much point to the rebuilding of the ruin, regarding it as more work than it was worth.[5] After retiring back to his home in Berkeley he was succeeded as project superintendent by NPS architect H.W. Whitsett, originally of the Regional Office in San Francisco.[6] Whitsett had transferred from CCC Camp

Cuyamaca in San Diego County and lived at the La Purísima Camp until
November 1936, when most of the excavation work was completed and the
foundation made ready to start construction on the padres' residence building.

Elevated Foundations

Ed Negus elaborated on one of the most difficult early problems of the restoration
project.

> When they started out, the order was to preserve the historical ruins. The
> biggest problem we had was to preserve all the old walls we could. A
> couple of attempts to preserve walls required an elevated foundation.
> Trying to preserve what we could of the wall, we lost a lot of it because
> the bottom part was completely disintegrated back to dirt again. We had
> to put in an elevated foundation to pump up and hold it, and it took two
> weeks for the concrete in the new foundations to harden. This was a pain
> in the neck even though we did it to several sections. It was far more
> work, and it would have been a lot simpler and better to level the whole
> thing off and work from the footings up.

Constructing elevated foundations (1935). [MISSION LA PURISIMA ARCHIVES]

Closeup of elevated foundations (1935). [MISSION LA PURISIMA ARCHIVES]

The old stone foundation of the residence building under the main wall, outside walls, and center wall, is four feet, three inches and an average of about five feet in the ground. We dug down there and laid some rock, sandstone which came from a couple of miles up the canyon. Originally, they were embedded in mud. They just took big stones and laid them right in mud and wedged them. Then they wedged in more stones and embedded them in good solid adobe mud. It was a far greater foundation than I ever realized. After the earthquake of 1812 shook down the first mission, I guess they wanted to be more careful. Their workmanship was far superior than what we were doing. So we had to go down through those footings, through the old foundation, and put an expanded pad in there to bring our reinforcing up from a pad underneath the existing foundation. Then we had to rebuild the foundation back up against the base. We had these raw recruits with the CCC boys that had to be put to work and trained at the same time. It was just one helluva big job.7

The First Adobe Bricks

Although he had no official permission to do anything more than preserve the ruins, Hageman had the foresight to direct the CCC crew to begin making new adobe bricks out of the rubble of the old bricks.[8] When the debris was cleared away from some of the old walls, they fell over, leading Hageman, Negus, and others at the site to conclude that preservation with concrete caps on the old adobe walls would not amount to much of a historical monument. Consequently, the first new adobe brick was laid in the reconstruction of the residence building on July 7, 1935.[9]

NPS historian Dr. Russell C. Ewing, a preservation advocate, objected to Hageman's rebuilding plans, and on September 9, 1935, wrote a formal report to the Regional Office in San Francisco. Ewing recommended that all reconstruction planning stop with the completion of the Residence Building because the old foundations possessed "great historic and archaeological significance in their present state." Ewing insisted that nothing be built unless it could be proven that it was an exact duplicate,[10] and Negus remembered a verbal exchange between Hageman and Ewing on that topic.

> Ewing's whole interest was checking authenticity with the artifacts and looking over Hageman's plans. Hageman would say, "It's only natural to assume that there was a window here." Ewing would say, "We are not assuming anything. You've got to have evidence that there was a window there before you put it in there."[11]

The Regional Office took no action on Ewing's report, so the rebuilding plan proceeded on its own momentum and the force of Hageman's personality. Ed Negus said, "Phil Primm was our district inspector and okayed a lot of the rebuilding work to keep it going, but it got to be what Hageman called a hot potato."[12]

Rebuilding Begins

By early summer, 1935, the most pressing of the major problems had been solved, with the plans and working drawings completed and approved by the State Park authorities and the Regional Office of the National Park Service.[13] Large crews of CCC enrollees began the seemingly endless task of manufacturing hundreds of thousands of adobe bricks and clay tiles. Others were engaged in gathering and preparing other structural materials, while still others were repairing the old, original stone foundations in preparation for capping them with concrete in readiness to begin laying the new adobe walls. On July 7, 1935, the first new adobe brick was laid by Phil Primm and construction of the first portion of the residence building began.[14]

Hageman had little historical documentation to work with. The Annual Report of Mission La Purísima for 1815, signed by Padre Payeras, provides this meager description of the structure under the heading "Buildings":

> The temporary ones have been undergoing repairs, propping up those made of posts which threaten to collapse, and they have built a wing one hundred varas [one vara is equal to 2.8 feet] in length, double row of rooms, with walls an adobe [brick] and a half thick and roof of tiles, which serves as habitations for the Padres with all the servants, guests, quarters, Chapel, and the rest for work shops.[15]

These few lines comprise the only written description of the residence building Hageman could find.[16] Evidently the padres were not nearly as interested in their physical accomplishments as they were in their spiritual work with the Chumash Indians.

Hageman reported the dimensions of the padres' residence building, the first to be reconstructed.

> The Residence Building is 290.17 feet long and has an overall length of 316.36 feet, including the open corridor at the north end and the massive stone buttress at the south end. In width, the building measures 51.28 feet, including the covered corridor on the east side and the open corridor on the west side, the total width is 79.47 feet. A central longitudinal wall divides the two rows of twenty-one rooms, and an arched passageway slightly over eleven feet wide extends through the building from side to side, near the south end. The building slopes downward a total of 3.87 feet from north to south and approximately a foot from west to east. The maximum height is thirty-four feet and the plastered adobe walls are approximately four feet and four inches thick.
>
> The tiled roof which covers the tile floored east corridor is supported by eighteen stately, plastered tile columns, nine of which are original and nine reconstructed. These columns are both chamfered and fluted at the corners, and with their white plastered sides and red fluted corners, are exceedingly graceful in appearance. They are constructed of rectangular, fluted tiles which are laid at right angles to each other at the corners. By

One of four mud pits where enrollees stomped a mixture of adobe mud and straw for making adobe bricks (1936). [MISSION LA PURISIMA ARCHIVES]

reversing each course, the entire shaft requires a single mold of tile. La Purísima is the only California mission where columns of this design appear.[17]

Making and Laying the Adobe Bricks

The magnitude of the task of reconstructing this building intimidated both the construction foremen and the CCC enrollees. In addition to those sections of the old walls which were saved, it was necessary to mold and lay 110,000 adobe bricks in the walls.[18] Each brick measured 24 inches long by 12 inches wide by 4 inches thick and weighed 65 pounds after drying.[19] Nearly 37,000 tiles were required to cover the roof, and 15,000 tiles measuring 10¼ inches wide by 10¼ inches long by 2 inches thick were required for the floors. Ed Negus complained that the soil was too sandy and the boys in the brickyard had to make three or four times more bricks than they used. Too many bricks broke after drying due to the sand content.[20] Each brick and tile was made by hand by CCC enrollees using nearly the same methods as the Chumash. Negus described the complexity of the scene.

[68]

Five enrolleess handling floor tiles in drying yard (1936). [MISSION LA PURISIMA ARCHIVES]

For every boy you had laying brick, you had a boy that was helping him by shoveling mud mortar to him. You had a mud box there, and then you had a boy wheeling mud up from the soaking pit down there where they were mixing the mud up. You had a couple of boys mixing mud and you had a boy wheeling it to one boy and another boy wheeling bricks to the brick layer to keep him from running and getting his own bricks. So for every boy laying bricks, you had four or five helping him. And if you had four or five laying, you had to keep them all straightened out.

[Engineering Mechanic Ralph] Ames made many more bricks than were used because the loss was considerable either in drying or handling. The broken pieces were cast into the mud pits and reused as mortar. Mud was always spilling down as the mortar was troweled around the bricks and one or two kids were always cleaning out around the scaffolding and putting the mud back into the pit. There were four mud pits for the Residence Building, and it took two days to empty one when they were laying brick. But it took three weeks to get the broken bricks soaked up so the mud could be stirred, so they worked from two pits while the other two were soaking. The mud couldn't be soupy, but had to be quite thick.

One section of a brick wall was done at a time in three layers about a foot thick. Then it was given a week to dry out. Ames wanted to go faster and build without scaffolding. But when it was built too quickly, the wall began to sag and push out of alignment. So Hageman made them work more slowly and allow the wall to dry.[21]

When the walls got up to four or five feet high, scaffolding became a major part of the work. On the main wall, the boys laid three layers of adobe bricks at a time. As they traveled along, they went about a foot high at a time, and when they came all the way around a given area, we had a scaffold. We had to raise the scaffold as we went around, and raise it again on the other side of the building. As we went around an area, it was almost a week before we got back to where we started to put the second layer on. During that time, the adobe would pretty well evaporate and dry out.[22]

When you came to the doorways, they didn't use the regular sized bricks. When you get to the doorways and the shape of the door and so forth, there are altogether seven or eight different molds of shaped bricks that had to fit in there. To get those bricks to fit, you didn't bring a brick out here and cut it off. You had to have a molded brick overlapping in such a way that you didn't have the joint one above the other.[23]

The Pugmill

During the first year, Win Keerl was the LEM in charge of adobe brick production. A graduate of Louisiana State University, Keerl had worked elsewhere for the National Park Service, and spent a long time experimenting with the adobe mud to get just the right mixture for floor and roof tiles.[24] The NPS brought in another LEM, Matt Mateus, to show the CCC boys how to mix mud and straw in a mudpit and how to mold the bricks.[25] It was a very slow process, and after a year, Win Keerl hadn't produced the amount of brick and tile that Hageman thought he should.[26] Keerl was transferred out and Ralph Ames was brought in. Ames had taken over for Negus on the Santa Rosa rock wall, and he devised a mill to mix the mud and speed up the brick making process. Negus described this innovation.

He got the pugmill from one of the local farmers and hooked it up to the axle of one of the trucks from the motor pool for power. The pugmill was like a long trough with twisting blades inside. When the blades turned, they mixed and pushed the mud and straw out into a wheelbarrow.

Using the pugmill (1936). [MISSION LA PURISIMA ARCHIVES]

Then the bricks were molded out on the ground. Ames revised this process until he got it the way he wanted it to work. A field half a mile from the mission had adobe dirt without too much sand, and this was added to the original bricks that had been stockpiled when the mission site was cleared of debris. If the mixture was too rich, the bricks would crack when they dried, so they experimented to get it right.[27]

The Camp newspaper, *The Voice of the Twin Camps,* also reported on the pugmill.

It was found that the clay being used contained small rocks, which caused the bricks to crack when they were baked, and it was therefore necessary to eliminate the pebbles. The rear wheels of a Park Service Chevrolet truck were removed and the axle turned at a right angle. The mixer sits on the bed of the truck, over the axle, which propels four paddle arms on the inside. The mixer holds almost 300 gallons. By mixing the clay and water in this contraption, the rock particles separate out and are released through

[71]

a trap door on the bottom of the mixer. After a few minutes of mixing, the clay is let out through a pipe to the pits. When the water has evaporated out sufficiently, the plastic material is formed into various shaped tiles. Several thousand tiles have already been made, most of them being square floor tile, with a few for the restoration of the pillars at the mission. In a short time the making of the roofing tile will be started, which will require skillful molding.[28]

Burning the Tiles

After drying in the sun, clay tiles destined for the roofs, floors, and water system were burned in a kiln. The tile shop workers made more roof tiles than floor tiles because they could reuse many of the original floor tiles after the mission was excavated. The kiln at Johns-Manville Company,[29] a quarrying enterprise in the Lompoc Valley, was used until 1938, when the enrollees at La Purísima built their own kiln.[30] Enrollees constructed the mission kiln out of red bricks at the site of the present-day parking lot. The kiln used oil for fuel—the same oil Gilbert Ballesterose brought from Avila, the same oil used in the camp kitchen stoves and

Drying roof tiles in the tile shed (1938). [MISSION LA PURISIMA ARCHIVES]

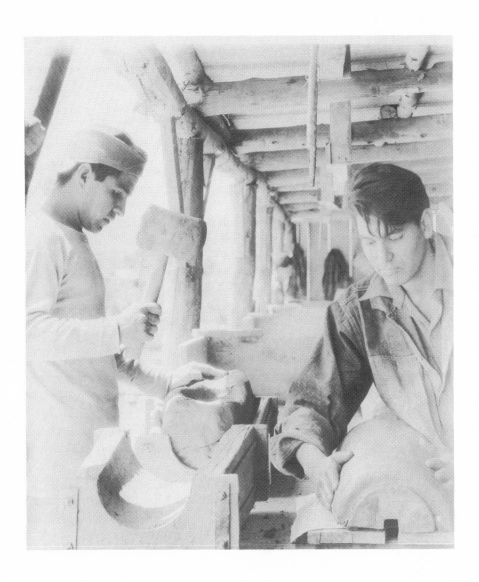

Two enrollees making *tejas* (roof tiles). Man on left is pounding clay into a wooden, semicircular form. Man on right is smoothing the clay over the semicircular wooden core. Tile shed (April 1936). [MISSION LA PURISIMA ARCHIVES]

inside the wooden buildings to keep the dust down.[31] Ed Negus insisted the aqueduct tiles of the Franciscan period were far superior and that the CCC men were never able to duplicate their quality.[32]

RAYMOND ELLIS

One enrollee came to be so skilled at the kiln that his enrollment period was extended because no one could replace him. Raymond Ellis spent two years as a tile burner and earned a nickname for it.

The first job he had when he arrived at La Purísima at age seventeen was hand rubbing tile in the tile shed.[33]

> Our quarry for the clay for the tiles was right on the corner of the mission property at first. Then the Lompoc Soil Conservation Camp found another clay quarry near Orcutt. So we hauled it in from there. Pappy Ames knew it would be right because its color was good. We crushed the pebbles from the quarry in a rock crusher and made it into dust for the floor and roofing tile.
>
> The adobe was different. It was just adobe earth mixed with sand, straw, and water to make mud which was molded into forms. In the pugmill, we put in two pitchforks of straw to two or three wheelbarrows of adobe dirt. Then we added the water to get the right mixture. We just kind of looked at it to see if it was right as the mud came out of the pugmill into the wheelbarrow. We set the adobe bricks in rows for about a week. We lost another ten percent of those to breakage, but we could reuse that. We would throw the broken adobe brick back into the pugmill and grind it up again into mud.
>
> We pressed out the tile, then we would hand rub it on both sides while it was still wet. One wet tile weighed about thirty-five pounds. We had a bucket to dip our hands in to rub it smooth. The idea was to make it like the original, not like modern manufactured roofing tile.
>
> Mr. Ames was a civil engineer and would come in each morning and make up the schedule for how much brick and tile we were going to need that day. He was soft spoken and really knew what he was doing. We called him "Pappy" Ames. He always wore Army olive drab pants and a hat like the old time cavalry officers used to have. He drove a 1937 Lincoln Zephyr, and came in at 7:30 every morning to set up the schedule for 120 roof tiles, or whatever we needed that day.
>
> We set the adobe bricks out in rows to dry in the tin tile shed. We inspected every clay tile and didn't burn it unless it was a good tile. It took

about a week for the clay tiles to dry out enough before we burned them. After it was burned, one roof tile weighed about sixteen pounds. The bricks took longer to dry when it rained, but we really didn't have much foul weather. I don't remember us losing any brick on account of the weather.

I got nicknamed "Firebug" because I burned the tile. I never fell asleep and never lost any tile. Mr. Ames made me a crew leader in the tile shed. Before me, we had a man operating the kiln and he let the clay get too hot and it melted in there. When you melt it, it's a heckuva job to chip it out of the oven. When you burn tile, you have to watch the color. We could tell by the color of the tile itself how close it was to the melting point. You had to watch it for twenty-four hours and check through the peep hole in the oven. It took about twelve hours to get the oven up to the right temperature, I think about 2,200 degrees. So it took about thirty-six hours to do a burn. We had a gauge, but that wasn't always true. You had to watch the color. The cook would send me ham sandwiches when I worked all night. Boy, I can still taste those ham sandwiches, they were so good!

We burned crude oil in the kiln. We had a tank truck and would go to Avila to pick up the oil. I had to sign for it, and rode along with Bali, the truck driver. Oil tankers deposited their cargo at the pier at Avila, and we purchased it. The oil sloshed back and forth in the tank on our truck because there were no baffles inside. It would slosh so much that the front wheels of the truck would lift off the road as we were driving, and we had a lot of trouble getting the oil back to camp. Boy, that Bali was quite a driver! We went to Avila about once a month.

There was a blower in the kiln for the flame to get hot, and I could turn the nozzle with a valve on the blower. So we could adjust the temperature as we watched the color overnight. When we loaded the kiln, we would use broken tile to space it inside for heat circulation. The roofing tile was narrow at one end and wide at the other end, so we would reverse the tile when we stacked it to create an air space between and the heat could get to both sides of the tile.

You would always lose about 10 percent to breakage because sometimes someone wasn't careful. And you can't reuse it after burning.[34]

In addition to his dollar-a-day wages as a tile burner, Ray Ellis became one of the more enterprising enrollees in camp and found two other ways of earning money while in the CCC.

I used to box. I learned to box at the gym in West Los Angeles. We could go to the ring set up by civilian promoters in Pismo Beach and box for a dollar a round. If it was a three-round bout, or a four-round bout, win, lose, or draw, you got three or four dollars. I was skinny and fast, and good in my weight class. I never got my nose busted.

The boxing ring in camp was behind the mess hall, and that's where you settled arguments. One time a guy called my mother a so-and-so and we got in the ring at camp. I got to him and beat him really good. Once I had him, I let him have it. But we were buddies from then on.

In my barracks, I ran the poker game. We played for nickels and dimes and I furnished the cards and the cigarettes. And I took 10 percent of every pot. I used to play poker as a kid and I did pretty good. We played five card stud, seven card stud, straight poker, nothing wild, and regular draw poker. Every night there was a game. It got me my other nickname of "Joker." And I used to loan the guys money at interest.35

Ellis had quit three paper routes and eleventh grade at University High School in West Los Angeles to join the CCC. His father had been a coal miner in West Virginia who brought his family to California during the Depression to find work. His mother had tuberculosis and Ellis had to go to work to help support his three sisters and one brother. To train for boxing, he would "run a block and walk a block" once a week to Venice where he had a buddy. Then they would swim together out to the *Rex,* a gambling ship docked in Santa Monica Harbor. They rested on the gangplank until someone came to kick them off, and then swam back. To lift weights, Ellis poured concrete into metal pipes and lifted those. He was in such good shape that he didn't gain or lose weight after he began working at La Purísima's tile shop.36

During World War II, Ellis served with the Marine Corps at Guadalcanal, then returned to Santa Barbara to work with his father in a family-operated upholstery business. That business later evolved into Ray's Top Shop in downtown Santa Barbara, specializing in upholstering auto and restaurant interiors, as Ellis retained his entreprenurial talents in later life.

The Abitudobe Experiment

While Ellis burned bricks and the adobe construction work proceeded, a new chemical was tested in the mud. Hageman agreed to tamper with the adobe mud mixture as an experiment. Negus remembered how it worked out.

After we got approval to rebuild instead of preserve, I think it was Standard Oil Company that tried to sell Hageman a material called Abitudobe, a bituminous asphalt product to mix with water and use in the adobe mud bricks so they would be water resistant and wouldn't erode away if rain hit them. The boys made quite a lot of those Abitudobe bricks out there in the brickyard, and they set them out to dry. They tried them along the walls of the chapel in the residence building.

Well, they tried the Abitudobe bricks down there and got up about six feet along the wall. But when they looked down, they saw it was squashing out. The bricks would not absorb moisture and the wet mortar mud went in there and wouldn't dry out. Hell, you had pockets of water and that mud was still wet even though it had been a week later. So they abandoned the idea entirely.[37]

Steel Reinforced Concrete

Just as the Franciscan padres reinforced their design of the second Mission La Purísima with sandstone buttresses and four-foot-thick adobe walls (instead of the two-foot-thick walls that had not withstood the earthquake at their first location), Hageman constructed modern alterations deviating from historic authenticity to ensure seismically safe buildings. He designed a steel reinforced concrete skeleton for the reconstructed mission buildings.[38] The adobe walls were built with internal square holes in which the reinforcing steel and concrete beams were placed. The beams were set into all the outside and center walls of the buildings, with the ceiling joists designed to take the lateral weight.[39] Hageman reported to the Advisory Committee why and how he broke from the authenticity rule on this feature.

In working out the structural details of the designs for the buildings, supreme importance was attached to factors of strength and permanency, including maximum resistance to earthquakes. These necessitated some divergence from the original methods of construction, as they involved the use of reinforced concrete columns, girders, and beams, as well as trusses and subroofs of modern construction. But as all these modern structural elements are concealed either within the thick adobe walls, or above the ceilings of the rooms, they do not involve any change from the original in the general appearance of the buildings.[40]

[77]

Negus described the hands-on experience with the beams.

The steel reinforcing was inside concrete poured at the mission. The steel had to be fabricated and tied at the mission. Every beam was numbered and listed with each different lengths and measurements. It was like a five-ring circus going on out there handling forty-five to sixty-five kids. Some were fabricating steel, some were building scaffolding and all that. Hageman had drawn it all out on blueprints, and I had to teach the kids how to do it.[41]

---

1. Wallace C. Penfield letter to Pearl Chase, November 2, 1934, correspondence files, Mission la Purísima Archives, Lompoc, California.
2. Frederick C. Hageman and Olaf T. Hagen, *Mission La Purísima Concepción—A Glance Through its History and the Story of its Restoration,* National Park Service, United States Department of the Interior (undated), Mission La Purísima Archives, Lompoc, California, p. 17.
3. *CCC Field Notebook No. 3,* Mission La Purísima Archives, Lompoc, California.
4. *Voice of the Twin Camps,* La Purísima CCC Camp, Lompoc, California, June 1, 1935.
5. Edward Negus Interview with Christine E. Savage, Lompoc, California, July 19, 1989.
6. *Voice,* December 6, 1935.
7. Negus Interview
8. Hageman and Hagen, op. cit., p. 17; Negus Interview.
9. Hageman and Hagen, op. cit., p. 19; Negus Interview.
10. Russell C. Ewing letter to Lawrence C. Merriam, September 9, 1935, correspondence files, Mission La Purísima Archives, Lompoc, California.
11. Negus Interview.
12. Negus Interview.
13. Hageman and Hagen, op. cit., p. 16.
14. Ibid, p. 19
15. Mission La Purísima *Annual Report,* 1815
16. Hageman and Hagen, op. cit., p. 16.
17. Ibid.
18. Ibid.
19. Richard S. Whitehead, ed., *An Archaeological and Restoration Study of Mission La Purísima Concepción—Reports Written for the National Park Service by Fred C. Hageman and Russell C. Ewing,* Santa Barbara Trust for Historic Preservation (Santa Barbara, 1980), p. 85.
20. Negus Interview.
21. Ibid.
22. Ibid.
23. Ibid.
24. *Voice,* November 1, 1935.

25. Ibid.
26. Negus Interview.
27. Ibid.
28. *Voice,* December 6, 1935.
29. *Voice,* January 21, 1936.
30. Civilian Conservation Corps, Los Angeles District, *News-Courier,* semi-monthly news-paper, Van Nuys, California, January 15, 1938.
31. M. Gilbert Ballesterose Interview with Christine E. Savage, Buellton, California, July 26, 1989; Franklin E. Hines Interview with Christine E. Savage, Los Angeles, California, July 21, 1989.
32. Negus Interview.
33. Raymond E. Ellis, Sr., Interview with Christine E. Savage, Santa Barbara, California, July 27, 1989.
34. Ibid.
35. Ibid.
36. Ibid.
37. Negus Interview.
38. Hageman and Hagen, op. cit., p. 18.
39. Negus Interview.
40. Hageman and Hagen, op. cit., p. 18.
41. Negus Interview.

7. "Spike" Camps

Fire Suppression Work

In addition to their normal assignments at CCC work sites, every camp was expected to release work crews for outside work, especially when called to suppress fires in the dry southern California terrain.[1] The summer of 1938 had more fires than usual. Locations included Refugio, Bakersfield, El Capitan, Bodger Seed Company, Guadalupe Lake Ranch, Buellton, and more sites in Kern, Monterey, San Luis Obispo, Ventura, and Los Angeles Counties.[2] In addition to his duties as construction foreman, Ed Negus was fire suppression foreman.

> As fire suppression foreman, I was the first foreman out on a fire. Trucks were always ready with tools and equipment, and twenty of my boys were picked from the crews. In case of a fire, all I had to tell them was "Get in the truck, we're going to a fire," and the other kids would take over while we were gone. We could be sent anywhere within a fifty-mile radius without having to notify the Regional Office in San Francisco. They came out with a memorandum that you couldn't go out on a fire without getting permission from the Regional Office in San Francisco if it was more than fifty miles away.[3]

Ray Ellis had a special problem when he was called for fire suppression duty. "I used to get poison oak so bad my eyes would swell shut. It was in the smoke. And I would get it bad."[4]

The Jolon Fire

Negus remembered a particular August 1936 fire in the Jolon area in Monterey County near King City,[5] outside the fifty-mile radius.

> I was at home when the call came in from the Regional Office for seventy-five boys to go to King City to fight a fire at Jolon. Walt Stewart said we should wait for confirmation because it was out of the fifty-mile

radius. They telephoned and okayed it, but Walt told them to confirm the order by telegram. He had had trouble with the procurement officer in the Regional Office before and wanted them to confirm this request by telegram. We only waited a few minutes before the call came from the telegraph office. They read the message to Walt and he said to me, "You're clear. Go ahead."

I took off with three truckloads of boys and went up to the fire, but by law we could only go twenty-eight miles an hour with everyone in the trucks. The orders read "Proceed to King City for gas and further instructions." The Regional Office no longer provided us with gasoline courtesy cards, so to go from here to King City in the trucks, we had to take along a dump truck with gasoline. I pulled into a Standard Oil station in King City and it was pretty late in the day. The boys began filling the trucks with gas and when they got through the gas station attendant asked if I had a courtesy card. I said, "No, just charge it to the Department of the Interior." He said, "You can't do that." I said, "Well, what are you going to do? The gas is already in the trucks."

So we had to call the manager of the Standard Oil station and he came out and I told him the score. I gave him the Regional Office's address in San Francisco, and he went and got some special forms I had to fill out for all the gas. He didn't know anything about the fire at Jolon and told me to go on up to the Associated Oil Station several blocks away. We left and all the other fire suppression crew trucks were at that station. It was the one I should have gone to but I didn't know it because I went according to the orders on the telegram. They directed me to the fire and we were out there for two or three days. I filled up with gas again before we left there.

Five or six months later, Vee Smith received a letter from the Regional Office wanting to know what right I had to charge gasoline to the Department of Interior. Vee was new as La Purísima's project superintendent then, and came out of his office down to where I was working and asked me if I knew anything about charging gas to the Department of Interior in King City on such-and-such a date. As I stood there thinking, he said, "Must have been a fire. Was it a fire?"

I said, "Yes, it was the Jolon fire and I charged gas at the Standard Oil station in King City."

"Did you have authorization?"

"Yes. Walt Stewart made me wait for confirmation of orders to proceed with a telegram."

"Do you have the telegram?"

I told him it should be in the office files, and he began searching for it. Vee had been a CCC camp superintendent for the National Park Service for a long time, and when he found that telegram, he said, "It's just what I've been waiting for all these years." He answered the Regional Office with a four-page letter about their orders and memorandums. He was an outstanding superintendent because of his ability to write reports. He wrote in a very polite way, but he told them off. Here they had issued orders and confirmed them, and then they wanted to know why I charged gas.[6]

Morro Bay Spike Camp

Because of less strict regulations in CCC extension camps, only the best of the enrollees from the La Purísima Camp were sent to construct the state park and boat slips at Morro Bay, on the California coast in San Luis Obispo County.[7] When any camp sent a group of men out on a job too far for daily commuting, a "spike" or extension camp was established with Army tents and a small kitchen. Frank Hines went as a KP to cook for the men at Morro Bay, Harry Davis drove the crew up there, and Robert Zaragoza was assigned to build a stone gutter around the Morro Bay golf course.[8] It was the only time Zaragoza got hurt while in the CCC.

I was breaking rock with a three pound hammer and I hit my finger. They didn't have a doctor in the spike camp, and my finger turned black and blue. I had to wait until the next day to see a doctor. I couldn't sleep, my finger hurt so bad. They brought me back to the main camp in Lompoc in a supply truck, but the doctor wasn't in. The medical assistant had to cut my finger open without an anesthetic. It hurt, but it had to be done.[9]

---

1. United States Department of Agriculture, Forest Service, *CCC Administrative Handbook, Region 5*, (Washington, D.C., October, 1938), p. 214-E. Located in the Archives of the Los Padres National Forest Headquarters, U.S. Forest Service, Goleta, California.
2. Civilian Conservation Corps, Los Angeles District, *Official Annual*, Ninth Corps Area (Van Nuys, California, 1938), p. 81.
3. Edward Negus Interview with Christine E. Savage, Lompoc, California, July 19, 1989.
4. Raymond E. Ellis, Sr., Interview with Christine E. Savage, Santa Barbara, California, July 27, 1989.

5. Civilian Conservation Corps, Los Angeles District, *News-Courier,* semi-monthly newspaper, Van Nuys, California, September 1, 1936.
6. Negus Interview.
7. Harry A. Davis Interview with Christine E. Savage, Claremont, California, July 22, 1989.
8. Franklin E. Hines Interview with Christine E. Savage, Los Angeles, California, July 21, 1989; Zaragoza Interview; Davis Interview.
9. Zaragoza Interview.

8. Camp Changes

CCC Camp Revamped

After the first year, many changes in personnel and facilities occurred in the Santa Rosa CCC Camp. In December 1935, Captain James Anderson became commanding officer of Company 1951, relieving Captain Clinton.[1] Negus recalled that no one regretted Clinton's departure. "He was Army spit and polish and very inconsiderate of the kids. He was transferred to the veterans' CCC camp at Somis, but was finally kicked out of the Army for misappropriation of materials."[2] Captain Anderson remained until July 1, 1936, when Lieutenant Kurt N. Heyne took over command.[3] Heyne remained with the company until February 1937. The Army continued to rotate commanders and adjutant officers in each CCC camp across the nation to provide them with a maximum of training placements.[4]

The biggest change for the enrollees was their relocation from forty Army tents in front of the mission ruin into wooden barracks on the mesa behind the reconstruction site. In August 1935, Reserve Army First Lieutenant Claus A. Tornell of the Quartermaster Corps was assigned as construction officer and

Twin Camps, established on a mesa overlooking the mission site. Note partially completed residence building at lower left (1936). [MISSION LA PURISIMA ARCHIVES]

[84]

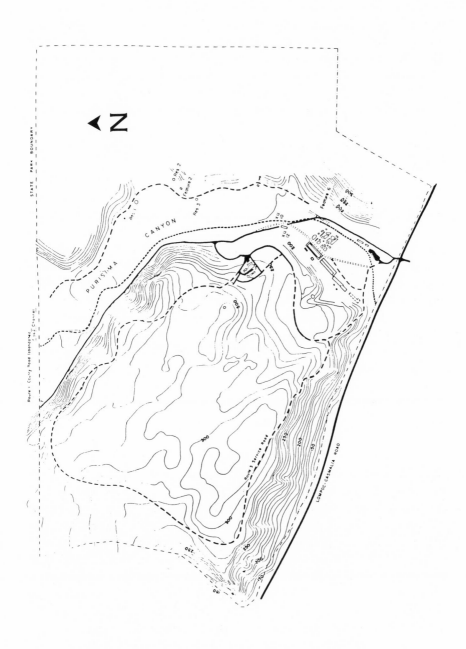

General site map. [MISSION LA PURISIMA ARCHIVES]

charged with the building of a new CCC camp on the hill overlooking the mission.⁵ Negus remembered Tornell. "His brother and father were in the construction business in the Bay Area, so he was very interested in the construction of the mission. He was level-headed and darn good."⁶ The four buildings which had been constructed at the original camp site were moved up the hill and set into place. Other wooden buildings were erected to house Company 1951, which maintained an average strength of 170 men throughout the reconstruction project. Two adobe buildings were built in the CCC camp as residences for the company commander and staff. The name of the camp was changed at this time from Santa Rosa Camp to La Purísima Camp.⁷

The Lompoc SCS Camp

CCC Company 2950, called Lompoc Camp, was formed April 11, 1936, under the supervision of the Department of Agriculture's Soil Conservation Service.⁸ Their assignment was to build check dams, water flumes, baffle plates, irrigation and contour ditches, and similar projects in the agricultural Lompoc Valley. The men were transported from the Fort MacArthur CCC processing center in San Pedro to their new camp, also located on the mesa behind Mission La Purísima. The combined CCC camps were like fraternal twins on top of the mesa, doing separate work projects with completely different supervision agencies, but sharing certain Army personnel and some facilities. They were referred to afterward as the Twin Camps. An advance cadre from CCC Company 1969 at Moor Park, later disbanded, was on hand to greet the new men of Lompoc Camp.⁹

The commanding officer of Company 2950 was Lieutenant Tornell, who was also the construction officer building the adjoining La Purísima Camp. Tornell served as mess officer for the Twin Camps as well.¹⁰ Reserve Army First Lieutenant Edgar A. Roehm of the Medical Corps served as the doctor for both camps. He provided medical care until May 1936, when he was replaced by Reserve Army Captain Forest E. Fleming, also of the Medical Corps, who was transferred from Company 903, Camp Angelus Crest.¹¹ One of the enrollees in the Lompoc Camp's Company 2950 was La Purísima's surveying enrollee, Frank Hines.

> It was the hardest work I'd ever done in my life and it gave me a great deal of respect for men who work with their hands. We had an all-white barracks for the truck drivers and an all-Chicano barracks for the workers. It was more segregated than the La Purísima Camp.

[86]

I remember one instance when the truck drivers insisted on sitting by themselves at their own mess table and not allowing any Chicanos to sit with them. Why the supervisors allowed that segregation to take place, I don't know. It didn't happen in the La Purísima Camp, but it did happen in the Lompoc Camp. This particular day, all the seats were taken in the mess hall for supper except for one empty seat at the truck drivers' table. A young Chicano sat down to eat there and they forced him to stand up. He was so insulted that he stalked out of the mess hall.

As soon as mess was over and the men returned to their barracks, a race riot broke out. The Chicanos began to holler "La Raza! La Raza!" [an ethnic rally cry] and they came pouring out of their barracks and stormed into the truck drivers' barracks. There were fist fights for half an hour until Captain Tornell and the barracks leaders finally got everyone calmed down. But there were plenty of bloody noses and other injuries. Some of the leaders of the truck driver group were from Texas and Oklahoma and they simply thought they were better than any Chicano. But at the La Purísima Camp, it was integrated and there were no race riots.[12]

The Twin Camps' Routine

Each day, the men of the Twin Camps came together for certain events orchestrated by the Army. Reveille was at 6:00 A.M., with the voice of a staff sergeant on the Twin Camps' loudspeaker crying, "Rise and face the glories of the newborn day," causing many groans inside the barracks.[13] Breakfast was served at 7:00 A.M., and everyone who was not ill was expected to attend assembly and the flag salute on the Twin Camps' parade ground at 8:00 A.M.[14] At this time, the company commander made various announcements and then dismissed the men to their work assignments. Company 2950 climbed into Department of Agriculture trucks to be transported to whatever worksite they were assigned that day. Company 1951 walked down the hill to the mission site.[15] Frank Hines discreetly described some of the rivalry between the two camps.

As the Lompoc Camp trucks passed the La Purísima men walking down the hill each morning, they gave each other a stiff finger salute. Sometimes the salute took the form of a two-fisted yanking motion. The men would get pretty energetic about it. It was a great way to start the day![16]

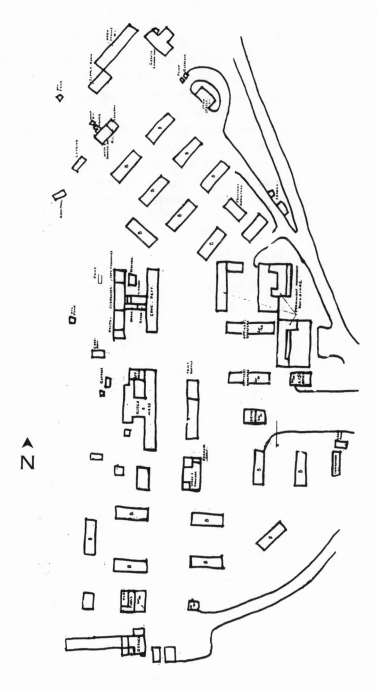

Plan of the Twin Camps: Company 1951, lower half, and Company 2950, upper half
(1936). [MISSION LA PURISIMA ARCHIVES]

The Twin Camps' kitchen staff served hot lunches at noon, and work resumed at 1:00 P.M. At 4:00 P.M., the supervisors called a halt to work for the day, the men returned to camp for showers, and assembled on the parade ground for retreat at 5:00.[17] Supper was served at 6:00.[18] Evenings were the time when the CCC boys could visit each other in the barracks, play illegal-but-tolerated poker games, take classes, read, walk into Lompoc for a movie, listen to the radio, play billiards in the recreation hall, and write letters. Most were too tired from the day's work assignment to do anything strenuous. Taps was sounded at 10:00 P.M. by camp bugler Alfred Cusick, who "murdered it with flat notes" according to Balleste-rose.[19] At that time, all lights were expected to be off and barracks leaders conducted bed checks to see if anyone was missing. Hines related one of his most distinct memories of the Twin Camps.

> The first thing I noticed was how dusty the camp was because the
> company streets were just dirt roads. And it was windy on top of that hill.
> The barracks, mess hall and other buildings had to be oiled to keep the
> dust down. The oil stunk like hell but it was better than breathing the dust.
> Every two weeks, we took the blankets off our beds and hung them out
> and beat the dust out of them.[20]

Many men went home for the weekends, but for those who remained in camp, Saturdays were spent cleaning the camp area, doing laundry and maintaining the company's equipment.[21] Sundays were days of leisure with group sporting events such as boxing and baseball.[22] Monday morning's reveille caused the whole routine to begin again as the mission slowly began to reappear out of its own rubble.

[89]

RECOMMENDATIONS OR SUGGESTIONS
MADE TO COMPANY COMMANDER AND
PROJECT SUPERINTENDENT FOR THEIR
CONSIDERATION.

A ventilated receptacle constructed for stale bread storage.

* * *

Stove pipe in Barrack B to be riveted with steel screws.

* * *

Fire buckets to be distributed as per regulations, including installation of two at men's latrine.
    NOTE: A new supply of buckets just received yesterday. No
          chance yet to distribute.

* * *

Tobacco receptacles installed in reception hall, as a fire safety
measure.
    NOTE: Exchange Steward said he had removed cans because of dam-
          aged condition, and that new and better ones were under
          construction.
                        * * *

A suggestion box installed in the recreation hall.

* * *

Prophylaxis to be sold at cost or less.

* * *

One or two sand buckets installed near kitchen ranges for use in
connection with grease fires, and Potts distillate heater.

* * *

"No Smoking" notices to be posted at both Army and State Park garages.

* * *

All sand barrels to be covered, for protection against rain. (Sand
muddy today).
                        * * *

A.W.S.

A. W. STOCKMAN
Special Investigator

1937 Camp Inspection Report.

ADDITIONAL REMARKS

SANITATION
Kitchen: Grease trap - pipe line - battery of three cesspools -
        seepage complete.

Bath House and Showers: Grease trap - pipe line into automatic
        flushing system in enrollees' latrine.

Enrollees Latrine: Automatic flushing system into battery of cess-
        pools with septic action.

Infirmary and Officers quarters (both camps), and quarters of
        technical staff (both camps) have flush toilets which
        empty into one larger septic tank.

Garbage: Collected daily by hog rancher.

Water: Good and supply plentiful. Only shortage is when pump machinery
        breaks down, which happens occasionally, due to age of
        equipment.

AREA
Located on mesa bordering La Purisima Canyon, within boundaries of
La Purisima State Owned Monument - 4½ miles from Lompoc, Calif -
on paved county road- elevation about 250 ft. - 14 miles from Pacific Ocean - immediate vicinity is covered with oak trees and native
brush.

Both winters and summers are mild.

Landscaping: Culivation of many varieties of flowers and catti,
        shrubs, vines, palm trees, hedges and large lawns.
        Very attractive. (This is a flora area.)

Grounds: Well policed.

LIBERTY PARTIES:

Friday, Saturday and Sunday nights to Lompoc, Calif., 4½ miles distant, for picture shows and skating rink. One enrollee per month
to Santa Barbara, 50 miles distant.

Athletic events as scheduled.

Special trips and merit trips to ocean beaches and various picnic
grounds and points of interest.

-1-

CLOTHING - SHOES

All issues satisfactory.

Eighteen pair of the new "Canvas-leather" gloves were received and issued yesterday. Wear about a month on tile work done by this camp.

Shoe repair said to be only fair.

Kitchen towels are washed daily account of limited weekly laundry supply.

ATHLETICS

Baseball diamond - basketball court - boxing arena - horseshoes - punching bag platform - horizontal bars, rings, etc.

Other gymnastics available at Lompoc High School, as well as tennis court.

MESS FUND - FEBRUARY 28, 1937

Cash surplus $603.05
Inventory value 480.94
        Total $ 1083.99

Nothing impounded at Corps.

GENERAL

Company Commander, who is relatively new on this assignment, has just bought a sound projecting picture machine. There is only one other in the Los Angeles District.

* * * * * * * * * *

The eight barracks are of the "56-man" type

* * * * * * * * * *

Park Service use tail gates for truck unloading ladders.

* * * * * * * * * *

Camp has commerical light and power.

* * * * * * * * * *

Educational facilities and infirmary are shared jointly with Camp Lompoc, SCS-9, which is immediately adjacent to this Camp!

-2-

Fire extinguishers, ~~encased~~, are with few necessary exceptions, located and encased on the outside of buildings, which I consider strategic.

* * * * * *

Considered from all points, and in every aspect, I would ~~consider~~ *classify* this a most excellent camp.

The present Company Commander has been on duty since February 1, 1937 with this camp, and the Acting Project Superintendent a few weeks longer. Cooperation between them is splendid.

I understand morale has increased since they took onver.

There were no complaints made to me by enrollees. Those whom I interviewed expressed satisfaction with all conditions.

In 32 camps in the District, this one ranked as follows: February 4th, January 7th, December 2nd.

* * * * * *

NEW DEAL ADOBE

1. Civilian Conservation Corps, Los Angeles District, *Official Annual,* Ninth Corps Area (Van Nuys, California, 1938), p. 77.
2. Edward Negus Interview with Christine E. Savage, Lompoc, California, July 19, 1989.
3. Civilian Conservation Corps, Los Angeles District, *News-Courier,* semi-monthly newspaper, Van Nuys, California, July 15, 1936.
4. Leslie Alexander Lacy, *The Soil Soldiers,* Chilton Book Company (Radnor, Pennsylvania, 1976), p. 198.
5. CCC *Annual,* p. 77.
6. Negus Interview.
7. CCC *Annual,* p. 77.
8. Ibid., p. 80.
9. Ibid.
10. Ibid.
11. Ibid.
12. Franklin E. Hines Interview with Christine E. Savage, Los Angeles, California, July 21, 1989.
13. Ibid.
14. Hines Interview; Robert Zaragoza Interview with Christine E. Savage, Los Angeles, California, July 24, 1989.
15. Hines Interview; Raymond E. Ellis, Sr., Interview with Christine E. Savage, Santa Barbara, California, July 27, 1989.
16. Hines Interview.
17. Hines Interview; M. Gilbert Ballesterose Interview with Christine E. Savage, Buellton, California, July 26, 1989.
18. Hines Interview.
19. Ballesterose Interview.
20. Hines Interview.
21. Zaragoza Interview; Ellis Interview.
22. Ballesterose Interview.

9. Camp Life

Leave Passes, AWOL, and Desertion

Each week a list of those eligible for weekend leave was posted in camp.[1] A certain number of enrollees always had to remain in camp for fire suppression duty, and some were restricted from leave for breaking camp rules.[2] Approximately half the camp got leave passes on Fridays and went home for the weekend.[3] Any enrollee who missed bed check on Sunday night was considered Absent Without Leave, but no one came looking for any missing enrollees.[4] Three AWOL charges could be grounds for a dishonorable discharge from the CCC.[5] Enrollees did not recall many deserters, probably because such men quickly grew discouraged by the work and camp life and left shortly after arrival. Zaragoza said of them, "They were mama's boys who didn't want to get up every morning and make their beds. They weren't used to taking orders and couldn't stand the discipline."[6]

Payday

All CCC camps paid enrollees their $5 once a month in cash, less any charges for cigarettes, candy bars, or razor blades at the camp's tax-free store.[7] Enrollees who had been rated as Leaders earned $35 each month and got to keep the extra cash.[8] Men in debt from barracks poker games simply surrendered their earnings to their debtors and went without spending money for the month. On payday, the men were lined up before the Army paymaster in the recreation hall in the evening after supper. Except for gambling, there was not much in camp on which to spend money, and many enrollees saved it for weekend leaves.[9]

Payday was also the day of the monthly "short arm inspection" when the enrollees were checked for venereal disease. When the men were already lined up to receive their pay, they also received a medical exam.[10] Robert Zaragoza said, "If you didn't get the exam, you didn't get the pay."[11]

[95]

CCC Camp Newspapers

Santa Barbara County Supervisor and La Purísima Advisory Committee ex officio member Ronald Adam was also the editor of the *Lompoc Record*. He assisted the camp's educational advisers, Peter Quin and Lloyd Vye, in setting up a journalism class in camp one evening each week.[12] Out of this class grew a bi-weekly camp newspaper first called *The Voice of the Twin Camps* and later renamed *The 51-50*, which referred to the last two digits of each camp's number. It published sporadically beginning in November 1935, and the enrollee reporters, editors, and typists asked for the patience of their readers because their only dictionary was a 1913 edition.[13]

One of their first news stories was about the first 750 clay tiles that were burned for the mission in the Johns-Manville plant in the Lompoc Valley on Wednesday, November 13, 1935.[14] The paper reported on the wins and losses in various camp sporting events, and printed the names of the ever-changing military personnel, along with a handy insignia chart so the enrollees could tell a captain from a first lieutenant.

This Twin Camps newspaper was discontinued a year later in favor of sending camp news stories to the *News-Courier*, the newspaper published twice each month from the Los Angeles District CCC Office in Van Nuys. The *News-Courier* printed information from all twenty-four camps in the District which had been sent in by enrollee reporters. La Purísima Camp stories included a detailed description of enrollee Louis B. Slusser winning $87.50 at the Lompoc theater Bank Night.[15] When the assistant director of the National Park Service, Conrad Wirth, visited the mission site in 1936, the *News-Courier* quoted him as saying the reconstruction work was "the grandest project I have ever seen the CCC put on."[16] Also in 1936, the *News-Courier* reported the presence of cameraman Roger Barlow at La Purísima. Barlow was funded by another New Deal agency, the Federal Theater Project, and shot 1,600 feet of sixteen-millimeter film of the reconstruction activities, as well as of the CCC boys in their camp on the hill behind the mission.[17] The *News-Courier* elaborated on Barlow's work.

> The Federal Theater Project plans to make a number of films of CCC activities. Purísima Camp was the scene of the first and was so chosen because of the unique quality of the project and because of its significance in California history.[18]

The Motor Pool

National Park Service Foreman William Cassuth managed the fleet of camp vehicles in the motor pool located at the southwestern corner of the La Purísima Camp.[19] The motor pool served the requirements of the Army personnel, the NPS requirements at the mission reconstruction site, as well as the Soil Conservation Service needs in the Lompoc Valley. The vehicle collection included Dodge and Chevrolet trucks of 1930s vintage.[20] The Army trucks were covered with canvas canopies and had benches inside for human cargo. The five Chevrolet trucks had flat beds with four-foot-high stake sides to haul both men and materials.[21] The engine starter was operated with a foot pedal beside the accelerator pedal in those trucks. Most of the trucks had radios for use during emergency fire trips.[22] There was also a tank truck to transport the camp's oil from Avila, three dump trucks and an International six-cylinder tractor.[23] Three LEM mechanics worked full-time in the motor pool to keep the vehicles in top running order at all times so they could answer fire emergency calls at a moment's notice. One mechanic named Pratt was given the nickname "Grandma" because he was so taciturn.[24]

CCC enrollees were charged with keeping the trucks clean and driving other enrollees to a work site. At the work site, enrollee truck drivers were expected to stay near the truck and not perform the manual labors assigned to the other men.[25] They had to remain free to pick up and deliver materials at the site, or to transport an injured man to the camp infirmary, or to respond to fire emergency calls. It was considered one of the best jobs an enrollee could have in any camp.

HARRY DAVIS

First assigned to excavation work on the east side of the mission site, Pomona enrollee Harry Davis looked for artifacts for three weeks, but found nothing. Then he heard that a test for truck drivers was going to be offered to replace other truck drivers whose enrollment had expired.

> I had a kind of an edge on the other guys at the truck driver test because I had been driving the family car for four years. I also used to haul a neighbor's oranges to the packing house in his truck. This was very unusual among the enrollees because they were mostly city kids who didn't know how to drive. I was further back in the test line and could watch the other applicants and how they took their test. Some guys got in the truck and would zoom around. Bill Cassuth, the foreman, asked us to

ℌonorable 𝔇ischarge
from the
ℭibilian ℭonserbation ℭorps

TO ALL WHOM IT MAY CONCERN:

𝕿his is to ℭertify That * ___HARRY A DAVIS___ ___CC9-280853___

a member of the CIVILIAN CONSERVATION CORPS, who was enrolled

___OCTOBER 3, 1938___ at ___VAN NUYS, CALIFORNIA___, is hereby
   (Date)

HONORABLY DISCHARGED therefrom, by reason of ** ___ETS - NOT DESIRING TO___

___REENROLL.___

Said ___HARRY A DAVIS___ was born in ___LA VERNE___

in the State of ___CALIFORNIA___ When enrolled he was ___NINETEEN___ years

of age and by occupation a ___LABORER___ He had ___BROWN___ eyes,

___BROWN___ hair, ___FAIR___ complexion, and was ___FIVE___ feet

___FIVE___ inches in height. His color was ___WHITE___

Given under my hand at ___CAMP PURISIMA SP-29___, this ___THIRTIETH___ day
                         ___LOMPOC, CALIFORNIA___

of ___MARCH___, one thousand nine hundred and ___FORTY.___

RAYMOND C. BALL, CCC Co Commander, Co 1951 C.C.C.
         (Name)   (Title)

* Insert name, as "John J. Doe."
** Give reason for discharge.
C. C. C. Form No. 2
   April 5, 1937

Harry Davis's discharge certificate was typical. [COURTESY OF HARRY DAVIS]

RECORD OF SERVICE IN CIVILIAN CONSERVATION CORPS

**Served:

a. From 10/3/38 to 3/30/40, under WAR Dept. at Camp SP-29, California

Type of work Truck driver *Manner of performance Satisfactory

b. From .... to ...., under .... Dept. at ....

Type of work .... *Manner of performance............

c. From .... to ...., under .... Dept. at ....

Type of work .... *Manner of performance ....

d. From .... to ...., under .... Dept. at ....

Type of work .... *Manner of performance ....

e. From .... to ...., under .... Dept. at ....

Type of work .... *Manner of performance ....

Remarks: EDUCATIONAL QUALIFICATIONS: High School 4 years
OCCUPATIONAL QUALIFICATIONS: Laborer, 8 years, and as above listed

Mr. H. V. Smith, Project Superintendent, makes the following estimate of
enrollee Davis as a workman: "Satisfactory"

ENROLLEE HAS BEEN NOTIFIED THAT HE CANNOT AGAIN BE ACCEPTED FOR ENROLLMENT
FOR A PERIOD OF SIX MONTHS.

PAID IN FULL AS FOLLOWS:
Due U.S. for $ none
Due CCC Store $ 2 0 0
Due Co Fund $ none
Due Allottee $ 2 2 0 0 Clarent T. Johnson., CCC Subaltern, Co 1951Spec.
Due Payeee $ 6 0 0 Agt. to H.G. COYKENDALL, Lt-Col. F.D.

Harry A. Davis

Discharged: HONORABLY, March 30, 1940 at Camp Purisima SP-29, Lompoc, California

Transportation furnished from Camp SP-29, California to Los Angeles, California

RAYMOND C. BALL, CCC Co Commander, Co 1951 C.C.C.
(Name)   (Title)

*Use words "Excellent", "Satisfactory", or "Unsatisfactory".
**To be taken from C. C. C. Form No. 1.

U S GOVERNMENT PRINTING OFFICE   3—10171

[99]

drive around shifting from first to second, third, and fourth. So I got in the truck and I just eased it into first gear, then into second, then into third, and fourth. He said, "Okay, shift down." So I slipped the clutch to take it out of fourth, goosed the throttle a bit into third, and didn't make any noise shifting gears. So we got back after one turn around the shed and he said, "Stop here. What's your name?"

"Davis."

"Be here at 8:00 in the morning."

Bill Cassuth was a wonderful guy to work for.

They needed adobe dirt down at the pugmill to make the bricks for the walls, so I was assigned to haul it. While driving the adobe dirt down the road in one of the dump trucks, I found that if I took my foot off the throttle and turned the ignition switch off, and then turned it back on, it would go "pop." I saw another driver, Art Hunt, coming toward me and decided to shake him up. So I turned the ignition switch off, but I turned it off way sooner than I should have. I was going slower than I thought, and by the time he got along side of me and I turned the ignition switch back on, there was a terrible boom. I blew the muffler apart. After I dumped the load at the pugmill, I checked underneath and saw the muffler seam had split wide open.

There was nothing to do but start putting it back together. I grabbed a handfull of baling wire from the bales of straw they had brought in to make the adobe bricks and wrapped it up. Art Hunt arrived while I was under the truck and complained that his ears were still ringing. When we got back to camp, I had to tell Bill Cassuth. I said, "They don't make Dodge mufflers like they make Chevrolet mufflers. I noticed the seam on the Dodge muffler was coming apart so I wrapped it with bailing wire and it's as quiet now as it was before." Bill was no dummy—he knew what I did. But he never mentioned it. He liked the fact that I went to him and told him.[26]

Davis was nineteen years old, respected fifty-year-old Foreman Cassuth, and admired from afar his attractive young daughter. He enrolled in the CCC about six months after his father died because his family was suffering financially. His mother read a notice in the Pomona newspaper about Civilian Conservation Corps recruitment. She realized that the $25 Harry could send home every month would cover the $22.50 monthly mortgage payments for the Davis family home. He liked it so much, he re-enrolled twice.[27]

[100]

I got to drive one of the '34 Chevy trucks up to the mountains at Los Padres National Forest to pick up the pine logs that were placed as beams in the padres' residence building. The Forest Service had harvested some logs for us up there. On the first load, I carried back three 16 footers, two 14s and one 12 footer. Coming down out of the mountains with that load of logs, it was so steep and the brakes were so poor that I shut the ignition switch off in first gear, and kept my foot on the brake and the parking brake on just to keep that thing from rolling out from under me. The logs were so long that they overweighted the back end. The front end was so light that I had to go around a corner in stages. The front end would come up, then the wheels would make contact again and I could turn a little, then they would come up again. It was a hairy experience.

On that trip, I noticed that there was a lot of play in the rear end. I hit the throttle and it would hesitate a second and then take hold. When I got back to camp I told Bill Cassuth we needed to take a look at the left rear axle. In those days, the rear axles were tapered with a keyway, and the hub likewise. Evidently the nut on the axle was not tight, and instead of being square, the keyway had worn into a figure eight. That's what caused the looseness. Bill told me to just put a new key in there and that took care of that. All that was involved was to just pull the cotter pin and the nut and the washer off the axle shaft. I brought in another load with no problem at all.

After I got the logs to camp, they had to be hewn with an adze to cut the beams to size and make them look authentic. One of the boys cut his ankle very badly with the adze and I had to haul him up to the camp infirmary. Boy, am I glad that doctor and the corpsman were on duty, or I don't know what would have happened to his foot.

I was also the guy who got to drive the tractor down in front of the residence building each spring pulling the discs to turn the earth and make it look nicer. It took all day to do it. I went down the back road behind the mission and coasted down the hill the first time, but the second time I kept it in gear. But I'll tell you what, when you are sitting in the truck and you see your buddies out there with picks and shovels, you get an awful guilt complex. So we would sneak an extra shovel for the driver even though the crew leaders didn't want the drivers to work. When we were digging the adobe dirt to put in the dump truck, there were no crew leaders to tell me to stay in the truck. I took that extra shovel and helped out.[28]

Davis had distinct memories of his time in the La Purísima Camp.

I was first placed in A Barracks. When some of the enrollees in there were leaving because their enlistments had expired, they were packing up their belongings and someone packed up my boots. So I moved over to E Barracks where the barracks leader was a guy named Pershing H. Bliss. He was the toughest guy in the barracks, but the second toughest guy had to test him. He challenged Bliss to a wrestling match, and Bliss put him on the floor real quick. After that, we had a saying about him: "If you mess with Bliss, you get blistered." Nobody challenged him after that. On the days when we oiled the barracks, Bliss made us stay outside all day to let it soak in.

On Sundays I sang the bass parts to all the hymns at the Lompoc Catholic Church. I knew the songs from memory from singing at church in Pomona. There was little animosity from the Lompoc townspeople toward the CCC boys, even though they were mostly city boys. Lompoc was a very small, quiet farming community and the flat land in the valley was used to raise flowers for seed. I remember one day in late spring that was beautiful, clear and cloudless. I was driving along and could see both sides of the valley. The hills were covered with wild mustard and the valley was covered with every color of flower that you could imagine. I'll never forget the beauty of that day, and I've always felt privileged to see such a sight.

We were offered a test once to determine if any of us had skills that made us acceptable for employment at Lockheed Aircraft in Burbank. The camp boasted a plentiful supply of dependable workers and Lockheed was interested. I took the test and was one of ten sent to Lockheed to take further examinations. After that, the man at Lockheed asked me if I could come to work there. With a home in Pomona and no car, I couldn't think of any way to get to Burbank everyday, so I had to turn it down. If I had accepted the employment offer, the CCC would have given me an honorable discharge.

There was very little interaction between the men in the La Purísima Camp and those in the Lompoc Camp. Even when the different barracks organized softball teams, we didn't have the Lompoc Camp men on our teams. We only came together for mess, but we sat on separate sides of the mess hall. In the mess hall, the food was exceptional. I remember the spaghetti. They would put a big bowl of spaghetti on the table and slurp, it was gone! I went into that camp weighing 140. Three months later I weighed 163. They would always have a pie of some kind cut into eight pieces and some chowhound would always gulp down his food to get the largest slice of pie.[29]

Davis had an especially precise memory of a softball game that occurred fifty years ago.

It wound up being a pitcher's duel between E Barracks and A Barracks. I played left field. When I came to bat, I hit a grounder and the shortstop followed it. He got in a hurry and overthrew first base. The guy dropped the ball and I tore for second. The guy overthrew second, he dropped the ball and I tore for third. The second baseman threw it over [A Barracks Leader] Joe Brito's head, so I made it home. That was the only run scored in that game. It was E Barracks, one to nothing. There were no hits, one run and three errors.[30]

Davis remembered singing in a camp quartet and winning a carton of cigarettes in an entertainment competition among La Purísima's singers. He also played the clarinet in the camp's band which also included a trombone, drums, and a trumpet.

We got compliments on our National Anthem at retreat in the evening, but we weren't good enough to be invited to play at any dances. Roy Thornburgh was the best guitarist in camp. Every evening that Roy would get his guitar out of his locker, he had an instant audience. He played the Spanish fandango so well that we would ask him to play it again and again. The more he played it, the better he got, and the better he got, the more we would ask him.[31]

Davis spent World War II in the Navy as an aviation machinist's mate and was stationed in Hawaii after the war. Subsequently, he worked for a variety of aircraft manufacturers in Southern California ending up in the automotive machine shop field for twenty-five years because he had become such an expert with internal combustion engines.[32]

---

1. Raymond E. Ellis, Sr., Interview with Christine E. Savage, Santa Barbara, California, July 27, 1989; M. Gilbert Ballesterose Interview with Christine E. Savage, Buellton, California, July 26, 1989; Robert Zaragoza Interview with Christine E. Savage, Los Angeles, California, July 24, 1989.

2. Franklin E. Hines Interview with Christine E. Savage, Los Angeles, California, July 21, 1989.
3. Hines Interview.
4. Ellis Interview; Hines Interview.
5. Civilian Conservation Corps Headquarters, Ninth Corps Area, *CCC Instructions* (San Francisco Presidio, July 1, 1938), p. 66. Located in the Archives of the Los Padres National Forest Headquarters, U.S. Forest Service, Goleta, California.
6. Zaragoza Interview.
7. *CCC Instructions*, pp. 13-14.
8. Ibid.
9. Ellis Interview; Ballesterose Interview; Zaragoza Interview.
10. Hines Interview; Zaragoza Interview.
11. Zaragoza Interview.
12. *Voice of the Twin Camps,* La Purísima CCC Camp, Lompoc, California, November 15, 1935.
13. *Voice,* November 15, 1935.
14. Ibid.
15. Civilian Conservation Corps, Los Angeles District, *News-Courier,* semi-monthly newspaper, Van Nuys, California, August 15, 1936.
16. Ibid.
17. *News-Courier,* September 15, 1936.
18. Ibid.
19. Ballesterose Interview.
20. Ibid.
21. Harry A. Davis Interview with Christine E. Savage, Claremont, California, July 22, 1989.
22. Edward Negus Interview with Christine E. Savage, Lompoc, California, July 19, 1989.
23. Davis Interview.
24. Ibid.
25. *CCC Instructions,* p. 154.
26. Davis Interivew.
27. Ibid.
28. Ibid.
29. Ibid.
30. Ibid.
31. Ibid.
32. Ibid.

10. The Mission Takes Shape

Redwood Beams

The original beams for the residence building were hewn from wood in pine forests on nearby Figueroa Mountain.[1] For the church reconstruction, Hageman decided to make use of redwood logs from the Stephens Grove CCC Camp in Humboldt County. Hageman knew the Franciscan padres had been able to make use of some redwood in the roof construction because he had the remains of those beams authenticated in the biological laboratory of the College of Agriculture at the University of California, Berkeley.[2] To obtain the redwood for fashioning the new ceiling beams, the floor planks, and the material for the doors and shutters, five NPS trucks were dispatched three times during 1936 to Camp Stephens Grove at Dyerville in Humboldt Redwoods State Park where CCC enrollees had

Redwood beams, newly arrived from Humboldt County CCC Camp, to be used in La Purísima's reconstructed church (1937). [MISSION LA PURISIMA ARCHIVES]

Unloading redwood beams (1938). [MISSION LA PURISIMA ARCHIVES]

labored for months to harvest massive redwood trees and split the logs into sections. They supplied redwood fence posts for many parks from this location.[3]

Upon arrival at La Purísima, the beams and planks were marked out and enrollees, using only axes, broad axes, and adzes, hewed them to size, dressed them down, and installed them in the building. The handsome corbels on which the ceiling beams rest were carved by hand, using wood chisels, gouging tools, and mallets. Negus described Hageman's directions to the CCC woodworkers.

> The beams had to be adzed to make them look old. Some of the boys got so darn good at adzing that they smoothed them up too much. Hageman came along and said, "No, I want more tool marks. I want to see those adze marks." He was very deliberate in trying to be as correct as possible.[4]

Hines described his use of the adze.

> You straddle the beam and chip the surface with the tool. It required no great skill. If you've used a pick and shovel, you could use an adze.[5]

Ellis remembered how *not* to work on the roof beams.

[106]

Enrollee in foreground using adze on timbers. Three enrollees in background working on beams. View looking southeast (1937). [MISSION LA PURISIMA ARCHIVES]

One guy was sawing out on the end of a beam up on the roof, and he sawed it off. He fell down and broke his leg. We couldn't believe how stupid he was. It was on the second section of the residence building. What a dumb kid! They really ribbed him about that. After he came back from the hospital, he still worked with a cast on his leg.[6]

Roof Construction

From the early photographs of the residence building, Hageman determined that the roof sheathing, on which the tiles were placed, consisted of a variety of cane, similar in appearance to bamboo. This was the common type of tiled roof construction during the mission period. A large amount of the cane was located growing in the Santa Clara River bed near Fillmore. The National Park Service horticulturist, Ed Rowe, was able to identify it as *Arundo donax,* and found that it was evidently originally brought to Mexico from Spain by the early mission padres. A small crew of enrollees went to the river bed to cut several truckloads of the cane, which they brought back to La Purísima and used where the underside of the roof was exposed, under the eaves. Several cow hides were purchased from nearby cattle ranchers and the cane was lashed together and to the rafters with

Laying roof tile on padres' residence building (1937).
[MISSION LA PURISIMA ARCHIVES]

rawhide, as shown in the early photographs of the original buildings.[7] Then on January 21, 1936, the first roof tiles were placed on the north half of the roof of the residence building.[8]

Plastering the Walls

Obtaining an authentic look in the plaster finishing presented a special problem for Hageman.

> An examination of the original walls disclosed that, on those parts of the building that were sheltered from the storms, which usually swept in from the southeast, the plaster was composed simply of mud, troweled onto the adobe bricks. On the more exposed walls, however, and on the interior walls, the plaster was composed principally of a mixture of lime and sand and was bonded to the adobe bricks by means of *rejuelos,* or broken bits of tile pressed into fresh plaster which filled grooves cut diagonally across each other in the adobe. These same methods were followed in the

Exterior plastering with a rubbing trowel especially created to duplicate original plaster marks (1937). [MISSION LA PURISIMA ARCHIVES]

reconstruction, but when the plastering was begun, not knowing what else to do, modern plastering tools were used for applying the plaster.

The result was far from satisfactory, as this method failed entirely to reproduce the texture of the plastered surface which was so characteristic of the original adobe buildings. To overcome this defect, the staff architect [Hageman] designed and had made a small metal trowel, by reshaping an ordinary cement edger, which was patterned after one of the original stone trowels found in the ruins with bits of plaster still adhered to its edges. The experiment was a complete success and these small trowels were used for applying the finish coat of plaster to all the walls. They were later dubbed "rubbing trowels," because the enrollees would stand by the hour, rubbing the partially set plaster for all they were worth, until a hard, glassy smooth surface was produced.[9]

Ed Negus had a different memory.

I got married in 1936 and took three weeks off for my honeymoon. Someone else was supposed to be in charge of the plaster work while I was gone so it would look just like the original. They put plaster in the grooves and then they put a piece of tile in to make the next coat of plaster stick on contact. But they just went ahead and threw it in and that's not right. They were supposed to put mortar in there and put the tile in and pound them in there flat so that you had a very smooth job and save a lot of plaster later on. I told Hageman one day, "In wet weather I'm going to come up here and redo this and have it done right." But I never got around to it.[10]

Plastering the mission's exterior walls was the second assignment enrollee Frank Hines had at La Purísima after he finished surveying the water supply system.

I was up on scaffolding and had to cut a diagonal grid into the surface of the adobe with a hand axe. This grid was filled with mortar which held the plaster in place. If you didn't do this and tried to plaster directly onto the adobe surface, it would melt and the whole thing would slip off. The

Interior plastering required a grid of mortar to bond the plaster to the adobe walls (1937). [MISSION LA PURISIMA ARCHIVES]

mortar was a lime and cement mixture which became very hard and held into the grid. The plaster would bond to this and stay in place. Every wall in that mission complex is gridded to hold that plaster. Everyone had to learn how to do this so the crews could be rotated. They didn't want one crew having to do one thing all the time.

Plastering was the stinkingest, dirtiest job in the camp, working on that wall in the hot sun with a hand axe, chopping away at the adobe. It would bounce back in your face, and of course you were covered with sweat and it would stick to you. Depending on the amount of scaffolding, there could be as many as a dozen men working on one surface. We were forcing all of the exterior work as fast as possible, along with the roof tiling, in order to get it finished before the winter rains. The interior walls could wait.[11]

Color Pigments

During the archaeological investigation of the ruins, all the plaster fragments which showed evidence of having been colored were collected. Later they were analyzed and color charts were made up to serve as a guide for the decorative designs. Red was used extensively on the buildings, and the original water storage structures and fountains were almost invariably plastered on the inside with red or pink plaster. Hageman found the only authentic way to duplicate the color.[12]

During the excavation, a number of solid lumps of red pigment were recovered, varying in shade from a light pink to a deep purplish red. Samples of this material were referred to a geologist who was very familiar with the area. He was able to identify it as a red diatomite and to point out the location of the deposits. A crew of enrollees was sent out to gather approximately a thousand pounds of this material, which they packed out to the road on their backs for a distance of about a mile. It was sent to Los Angeles to be ground and was used for applying the dadoes [decorated lower walls] to the restored buildings.[13]

Woodwork and Hardware Handmade

The massive carved doors, the shutters, the stairs and stair rails, the chancel rails, choir rails, and other woodwork were all fashioned by hand and fastened together by wedged dove-tail or mortise-and-tenon joints, wooden dowels, or handmade iron nails. The patterns for the joints were determined by carefully taking apart

Enrollees pose in front of the wood shop (1938).
[COURTESY OF GILBERT BALLESTEROSE]

sections of some of the old woodwork unearthed in the ruins of the buildings.[14] One day the CCC carpentry workers needed to move a shed, and Ed Negus watched them.

> The temporary carpenter shop was beside the temporary nursery in front of the shops and quarters building. It was an open shed that we needed to move from north of the residence to down in front of the church to become another tool shed. About ten of the kids were chosen to pick up and carry the structure. They set it down to rest at the halfway point, and then picked it up again. The kids in the back were in a bigger hurry and no one was counting cadence as they moved. Almost at the end, the boys in the back sat their end down first, and the building fell to pieces.[15]

All the buildings that were not moved up on the mesa for the CCC camp became temporary sheds at the mission site. Hines remembered the carpentry workers in one of those sheds.

Room 9 **Almacen de Herramientas** (Tool Room)
  10 hoes with handles in SW corner
  7 home-made shovels with handles, against W wall
  3 picks with handles, against W wall
  6 axes with handles, against W wall
  2 hatchets with handles, against W wall
  1 large chest against S wall west of door
  2 machetes hanging on a peg on S wall
  5 sickles hanging on a peg in S wall
  3 wooden pitchforks against S wall west of chest
  2 wooden plows in SE corner
  2 ox-yokes, Spanish type
  2 ox-goads
  3 pack saddles, sparejo type, in NE corner
  3 double pack-bags of leather for same
  3 pack ropes with wooden hooks for same

Room 10 **Cuarto o Celda de Fr. Payeras** (Room or cell of Father Payeras)
  1 cot, rawhide covered, in NE corner against N wall. Mattress
    (yerga tick stuffed with wool), 2 sheets, 2 handwoven
    blankets, pillow with case
  1 sheep skin for a rug in front of cot
  1 plain table against South wall, east side
  1 simple chair at table
  1 candlestick on table
  1 snuffer on candlestick
  1 breviary bound in vellum on table
  1 oil painting of St. Francis (San Francisco) on wall above table.
    Framed
  1 large crucifix, 16 or 18 inches high on west wall
  1 prayer stand in front of crucifix (?) (I am not sure Franciscans
    had this)
  1 simple wash stand against S wall, west side
  1 pottery wash bowl on stand
  1 water olla on floor beside stand
  1 towel on side of stand
  1 small mirror, plain frame over wash stand
  1 small chest, very plain, against N wall, west side of door
  1 toilet stool, closed type

Part of a thirty-page list of furnishings for the rooms at La Purísima originally prepared by Dr. Mark R. Harrington, curator of the Southwest Museum in Los Angeles. [MISSION LA PURISIMA ARCHIVES]

There were two men who were simply geniuses at woodworking. They reproduced all the doors and other carved work. They were very jealous of their domain and wouldn't let us stay over there for long.[16]

One of those geniuses was enrollee Gilbert Loya, the crew leader in the wood shop for three years, and the same barracks leader who showed Robert Zaragoza how to make his bed. He grew so skilled at making reproductions of mission furniture that Vee Smith wrote a letter of recommendation to Dr. Mark R. Harrington, curator of the Southwest Museum, who was able to find Loya further employment at Mission San Fernando.[17]

Similar to the woodwork, all the ironwork, including the cumbersome locks and keys, the heavy hinges, hasps, and latches, the iron and brass lighting fixtures, and all the exposed iron nails, were hand-forged by Valentine Goelz of Hessen, Germany, an exceptionally skilled metal worker especially employed for that purpose by the National Park Service.[18] He was assisted in the blacksmith shop by a CCC enrollee, Richard Barrios, whom he trained so thoroughly that Barrios was later able to successfully take over the task of making much of the iron work for the other reconstructed buildings.[19] Barrios spent his subsequent life working with ornamental iron, and Harry Davis remembered the level of skill Barrios achieved.

> Before I got into the CCC, I had seen a couple of blacksmiths at work. When I saw Richard Barrios, I was amazed at what he could do with a piece of iron. He was one of the best blacksmiths I have ever seen in my life. He took the ironwork relics, the door hinges, the latches, and other things, and he would duplicate them so perfectly it was amazing. His square nails were a work of art. He was tremendous.[20]

The padres' residence building was the only structure in the rebuilt mission complex that was wired for electric lighting, because the original reconstruction plans called for a full-time caretaker to live in two of the rooms.[21] In July 1937, Project Superintendent Vee Smith wrote a facetious letter to Valentine Goelz, who lived in Glendale. A problem had occurred with the electricity in two of Goelz's historically accurate metal reproductions.

> You know those two wall fixtures the ornamental blacksmith put up? Well, the damn things shorted and blew Walt Stewart out through the front door and smashed down a lot of Ed Rowe's hollyhocks—and Walt is mad and so is Ed and Walt says if we don't get them fixed he is going to yank them off and throw them away.
>
> Now Mr. Goelz, you know I would hate to have Walt do anything like that because it leaves big holes in the wall, and anyhow we haven't got anything else to put up in their place unless we cut the bottoms out of some cans and nail them over the holes and Fred don't think that would work because it wouldn't be authentic.
>
> So I ask you, Mr. Goelz, what am I going to do unless you bring your tools and a keg of Schlitz and come up and fix those two fixtures before

Walt gets too mad and starts swearing right in the chapel. If you can't get
Schlitz, most any good kind of beer will do that there is a kick in.

As ever, your friend, Hach Heil and Prosit!

H.V. Smith, Superintendent, La Purísima Camp[22]

Furniture Making

As work on the building progressed, the Advisory Committee felt that the
addition of some articles of furniture in the various rooms would add to their
character and interest. Accordingly, measured drawings and photographs were
made of original benches, chairs, tables, and chests that still existed in other
missions from San Carlos to San Luis Rey. A small, select group of enrollees

Two enrollees carrying replicas of mission chairs constructed in woodshop behind
them (1938). [MISSION LA PURISIMA ARCHIVES]

under Construction Foreman Walt Stewart's supervision was put to work making reproductions of these articles.[23] Fortunately, one of the original benches from La Purísima was located and loaned to the State of California by its owner, Frank J. McCoy, proprietor of the nearby Santa María Inn.[24] Reproductions of this bench were made in the La Purísima woodshop.[25] Later, Dr. Mark R. Harrington, one of the Advisory Committee's consultants and curator of the Southwest Museum in Los Angeles, compiled a complete list of the articles needed to furnish all the rooms of all the buildings, along with the locations of many of the originals.[26] Reproductions of most of these articles were made by the enrollees. Hageman described the back-breaking work involved in making the pieces authentic.

> The material for making the furniture was obtained from trees felled in the nearby pine forests by the enrollees. The logs were transported to camp, placed over a saw-pit, and whipsawed into crude planks, one at a time. Only by this method could the character of the old articles be reproduced. A few pieces were made of mahogany and magnolia, as were the originals.[27]

LEO MANDEVILLE

One enrollee who began working in the woodshop moved on to get a cushy job in the La Purísima Camp's administrative office behind the mission. Leo Mandeville remembered what happened after he tagged along with some Santa Barbara friends when they joined the CCC.

> I had woodworking experience in junior high school, so they took me into the woodshop and had me making the bars and the window frames for the mission. I was a "chisel knocker," making the square holes for the bars to go into with a chisel and mallet. It took almost a week to finish one. Then they had me stripping the bark off the new cottonwood logs lying in the shade behind the mission. I used an axe for that. After that they put me on chopping the hardened adobe brick to fit the wooden door of the church building. So about that time I said, "The heck with this." They needed someone who could type in the camp office, and I had taken typing in school, so I transferred up there.
>
> I mostly typed government forms in triplicate for the camp supervisors, no correspondence. The office personnel had their own barracks away from the others with private showers. It was more or less the elite there. I typed sick leave records, pay records, requisitions for the camp supplies,

and leave requests on an old typewriter. I could go about sixty words per minute. There were six private rooms in our barracks and I had to share my room with only one other man. Everyone got along really well in that barracks because they knew they had it good. They didn't gamble or steal. We even had our own laundry there.

I was only seventeen when I joined, and didn't care much for living in the other barracks with twenty men. They never even inspected the barracks of the office personnel. We weren't bothered by anything like that. One thing I learned in the office was how to handle carbon paper. How to turn carbon forms in a typewriter. You put the paper and carbons in and you type. The first line is real beautiful, the second one down a little bit, and the third one down a little bit more. You have to roll them up, you know. That's one thing they didn't teach me in high school is how to do carbons. The other guys wore their blue jeans and fatigues at the mission, but we wore our CCC uniforms in the office. They were Army-issued khaki, and we called them "suntans."[28]

Mandeville's father had run a grocery store, but died in 1934. His mother operated a small hotel to support the family, and he had quit high school to help her out. He thought he might be able to finish his education in the CCC, but only took a few vocational classes while enrolled. On weekends he often went home to Santa Barbara to see his girlfriend, or walked into Lompoc for church services.[29] He described a low-key military presence in the La Purísima Camp.

My mother sent me to St. Catherine's Military Academy in Anaheim when I was a youngster. I think she wanted to have more control over what I was doing. That was much more military than the CCC. In the CCC we didn't have any about face, left face, saluting, or marching. We only had to fall in and stand at attention sometimes for assembly. Except for the company commander, I don't really remember the military officers.[30]

---

1. Richard S. Whitehead, ed., *An Archaeological and Restoration Study of Mission La Purísima Concepción—Reports Written for the National Park Service by Fred C. Hageman and Russell C. Ewing,* Santa Barbara Trust for Historic Preservation (Santa Barbara, 1980), p. 189.
2. Ibid, p. 188.

3. Frederick C. Hageman and Olaf T. Hagen, *Mission La Purísima Concepción—A Glance Through its History and the Story of its Restoration,* National Park Service, United States Department of the Interior (undated), Mission La Purísima Archives, Lompoc, California, p. 20a; Civilian Conservation Corps, Los Angeles District, *News-Courier,* semi-monthly newspaper, Van Nuys, California, June 8, 1936.
4. Edward Negus Interview with Christine E. Savage, Lompoc, California, July 19, 1989.
5. Franklin E. Hines Interview with Christine E. Savage, Los Angeles, California, July 21, 1989.
6. Raymond E. Ellis, Sr., Interview with Christine E. Savage, Santa Barbara, California, July 27, 1989.
7. Hageman and Hagen, op. cit., p. 23.
8. *News-Courier,* February 1, 1936.
9. Hageman and Hagen, op. cit., p. 21-22.
10. Negus Interview.
11. Hines Interview.
12. Hageman and Hagen, op. cit., p. 22.
13. Ibid.
14. Hageman and Hagen, op. cit., p. 20a.
15. Negus Interview.
16. Hines Interview.
17. H.V. Smith letter to Mark R. Harrington, July 16, 1940, correspondence files, Mission La Purísima Archives, Lompoc, California.
18. *News-Courier,* October 1, 1936.
19. Harry A. Davis Interview with Christine E. Savage, Claremont, California, July 22, 1989; Hines Interview; Ellis Interview.
20. Ibid.
21. *Development Outline for La Purísima Historic Monument* (specifications to accompany architectural drawings, author not named), undated, p. 9. CCC Files, Mission La Purísima Archives, Lompoc, California.
22. H.V. Smith letter to Valentine Goelz, July 28, 1937, correspondence files, Mission La Purísima Archives, Lompoc, California.
23. Hageman and Hagen, op. cit., p. 23.
24. Whitehead, op. cit., p. 176.
25. Hageman and Hagen, op. cit., p. 24.
26. Mark R. Harrington, *Furnishings,* La Purísima Mission State Historic Park, April 20, 1939, Mission La Purísima Archives, Lompoc, California.
27. Hageman and Hagen, op. cit., p. 24.
28. Leo E. Mandeville Interview with Christine E. Savage, Santa Barbara, California, July 17, 1989.
29. Ibid.
30. Ibid.

11. The Site Refined

Residence Building Dedicated and State Park Opened

On Labor Day, September 6, 1937, 1,500 Santa Barbara County residents attended a ceremony to dedicate the padre's residence building and officially open the state park to the public. State officials named it La Purísima State Historical Monument, and the principal speaker on opening day was chairman of the State Park Commission, Joseph R. Knowland. The National Park Service and the CCC enrollees had taken approximately two years to reconstruct the building, which was about the same amount of time as it had taken the Franciscans and Chumash beginning in 1813. For the dedication ceremony, they built a temporary thatch-covered ramada beside the west wall of the residence building, where a basket picnic took place.[1]

Santa Barbara County Supervisor and ex-officio Advisory Committee member Ronald Adam was master of ceremonies and introduced Clarence "Pop" Ruth, a Lompoc school teacher who was president of a group of local citizens known as the La Purísima Mission Association. Ruth was gratified by the large audience, and proposed holding an annual fiesta at the mission every Labor Day which would be organized by his Association. Fr. Augustin Hobrecht, O.F.M., expressed appreciation from the Franciscans at the Santa Barbara Mission. The choir from Santa Barbara's Franciscan Seminary, St. Anthony's, sang a chant as they walked down the building's corridor, deliberately recreating a sight and sound common at the mission over one hundred years before.[2]

J. Lee Bossemeyer represented the National Park Service, and praised the CCC boys for their work. He pointed out that many of the La Purísima enrollees were being placed in private employment after their discharge from the mission project, which he saw as indicative of the quality of work experience and instruction they received while in the CCC. After the food, songs, and speeches, Hageman and Smith gave everyone tours of the grounds.[3] For his admirable work, Hageman received a personal thank-you note signed by Wallace Penfield, Pearl Chase, Phil Primm, and Carleton Winslow.[4]

La Purisima State Historical Monument

Official Dedication
September 6, 1937

Official Program
of La Purisima Mission, Lompoc, California

12:30 to 1:00 P. M.
Band Concert, Lompoc Municipal Band

1:00 to 2:00 P. M.
Basket Lunch

2:00 P. M.
Supervisor Ronald M. Adam, Master of Ceremonies

"Star Spangled Banner" - Lompoc Municipal Band

Address of Welcome - Clarence Ruth
(President La Purisima Mission Association)

Music - St. Anthony's Seminary Choir

REV. FATHER AUGUSTIN HOBRECHT, O.F.M.
(Old Mission Santa Barbara)

Music - St. Anthony's Seminary Choir

MR. J. LEE BOSSEMEYER
(Representing National Park Service)

Native Daughters of the Golden West Representative

Introductions - Ronald M. Adam

Music - Santa Barbara Tipica Orchestra

HON. JOSEPH R. KNOWLAND
(Chairman State Park Commission)

Music - Santa Barbara Tipica Orchestra

Immediately following the program the National Park
Service staff will conduct a tour of the
mission buildings and gardens.

[MISSION LA PURISIMA ARCHIVES]

Believed to be dedication of residence building (Sept. 6, 1937). STANDING, LEFT TO RIGHT: L. Deming Tilton, director, Santa Barbara County Planning Commission; Ronald M. Adam, Santa Barbara County supervisor; Edwin Denys Rowe, National Park Service landscape foreman; Frank E. Dunne, Santa Barbara County forester; Harry Buckman, Santa Barbara County Board of Forestry; Frederick C. Hageman, National Park Service architectural foreman; Arthur L. Darsie, National Park Service engineering foreman. SEATED: Wallace C. Penfield, Santa Barbara County Planning Commission engineer; Lawrence Liebeu, National Park Service fire suppression foreman; Arthur Woodward, archaeologist, Los Angeles County Museum; H.V. Johnston, National Park Service superintendent of La Purísima Camp; Dr. Owen C. Coy, director of California State Historical Commission and chairman of Department of History, University of Southern California. [MISSION LA PURISIMA ARCHIVES]

Water Structures Restored

During 1938, restoration of several units of the water system was completed. These included the octagonal fountain, two lavanderias for washing clothes (one for the Franciscans and one for the Chumash), a stone aqueduct, and a large reservoir, all of which were in the garden in front of the residence building. All were constructed of stone and tile masonry, and the two lavanderias were encircled by flat slabs of stone on which the clothes were pounded. The lavanderia for the Indians also served as a bathing pool.[5]

About a quarter of a mile across the valley from the main building group stands the spring house. Water for domestic use at the mission was piped from this

Excavating original mission water system (1938).
[MISSION LA PURISIMA ARCHIVES]

building through a tile pipeline to the octagonal fountain. Hageman chose to preserve instead of reconstruct the spring house.

> Due to the interesting character of this little building, with its vaulted masonry roof, no attempt at complete restoration was made, but such preservative measures were taken as would check further disintegration.[6]

Gardens

To add to the historical and educational interest of the restored mission, a plot of about four acres, which included the three fountains directly in front of the residence building, was planted as a garden. It was not intended as a restoration of a mission garden (although elaborate gardens were known to have existed at some of the missions, notably San Luis Rey), but was instead intended as an exhibit of plants introduced to California by the mission padres and the early Spanish and Mexican colonists.[7] Since an exhibit of these plants alone would have been

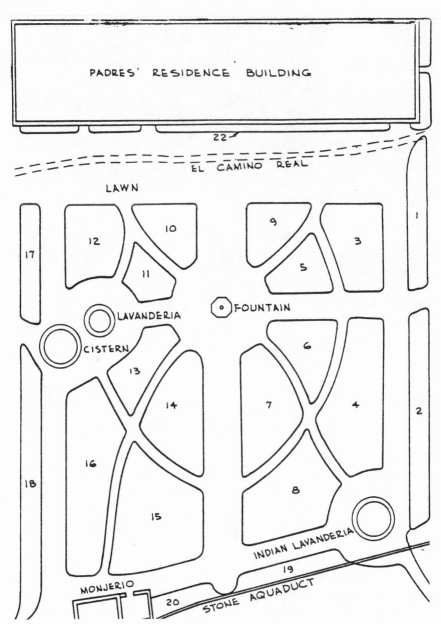

PADRES' RESIDENCE BUILDING

22

EL CAMINO REAL

LAWN

17
12
10
11
9
3
5
1

LAVANDERIA
FOUNTAIN
CISTERN
13
6
14
7
4
2
16
18
8
15

INDIAN LAVANDERIA
19
MONJERIO
20
STONE AQUADUCT

La Purísima garden designed by Louis Brandt, landscape architect for the National Park Service. Each numbered plot contained representative native plantings grown by Landscape Foreman Ed Rowe and his CCC work crew. [COURTESY OF COMMUNITY DEVELOPMENT AND CONSERVATION COLLECTION, UCSB LIBRARY]

disproportionately small by comparison to the building group, the garden was expanded to include a collection of some 250 varieties of native flowering plants and shrubs, many of which were used medicinally by the Spaniards, Mexicans, and Indians.[8]

The formal garden plan was designed by a group of National Park Service landscape architects headed by Louis Brandt from the Regional Office in San Francisco.[9] Forty-eight-year-old olive trees were transplanted from Los Olivos, thirty-five miles from the mission.[10] They were moved with their root systems enclosed in four-foot boxes, and a special tackle had to be devised by the CCC men to load the heavy trees on to the NPS trucks.[11] Palm trees were moved in from the highway right-of-way near La Patera Road a little west of Goleta in Santa Barbara County.[12] The La Purísima project's staff horticulturist, Edwin Denys Rowe, selected those particular trees for their aged appearance because he felt they added to the atmosphere of quiet serenity the garden was helping to create at the mission.[13]

Other mission plants such as pomegranates, figs, pears, pepper trees, grapes, and Castillian roses were propagated by Rowe from grafts, buds, and cuttings from original plants growing at different missions extending from Santa Clara to San Juan Capistrano.[14] By 1941, there were 306 varieties of native plants set out in La Purísima's garden.[15] The transformation from a barren, dusty bean field to a garden of surpassing beauty was astounding, and was due to the efforts of Rowe and the CCC enrollees he supervised. In a 1941 article for the California Garden Clubs, he said he followed a rule of "orderly disorder" in the garden.[16]

Horticulturist's Background

Ed Rowe was born in England and came to the United States in 1906, first settling in Detroit, and then in Santa Barbara. He worked as a gardner and eventually became well-known to the community's wealthier residents as a landscape architect. He landscaped the Royal Hawaiian Hotel on the Hawaiian Islands, but overextended himself and lost everything in the Depression.[17] Rowe was not experienced with California native plants, and spent time picking the brains of Ed Negus's wife, Martha, who was a school teacher with botany training from the University of California at Berkeley.[18] He educated himself well enough to develop a large nursery of native plants for the mission grounds. Rowe also grafted from fruit trees that dated from the mission period to bring back the old pear and apple orchards.

Ed Rowe lived at the camp, and Negus remembered that "he was always around the nursery. If people came out to see the place, he would drive them

Nursery stock lined up to southeast of residence building, north section partially finished and south section just begun. Potting shed at left of center (1936). [MISSION LA PURISIMA ARCHIVES]

around. He was always here even though he didn't have to be."[19] In April 1938, the Santa Barbara County Park Service Office recorded 2,267 visitors to the mission reconstruction project,[20] so Rowe's presence was critical.

Rowe's horticultural work at La Purísima was extensive, and in 1937 he employed sixteen enrollees as tree foremen, thirteen as tree trimmers, seven as gardeners, one nurseryman, forty-one laborers, and forty-eight equipment operators, for a total of 126 landscape workers.[21] Enrollees invariably remembered Rowe with fond respect and recalled he was the only foreman who never got dirty. Robert Zaragoza described him as "always wearing riding boots and britches, and he drove a LaSalle."[22] One enrollee in particular got to work very closely with him, an association that had a profound impact on the rest of his life.

SEYMOUR ADLER

Seymour Adler was born in New York City, but his family moved to California when he was six years old. His father, a furrier, needed a milder climate to improve his health after suffering through poison gas attacks in World War I, but he contracted pneumonia in 1928 and died. Seymour, the eldest son, quit eleventh grade and went to work in the city parks of Los Angeles through the National Youth Administration (NYA) for $18 a month. A friend on that job told him about the CCC where he could earn more money.

> I didn't stay in the CCC to take classes and get my high school diploma because it was more important to have the job and help out my mother and my sister and my brother. I hated relief, so I did what I could to help out the family. After my dad died, my mother couldn't take care of all of us, so she sent me up to a boys' home in Azusa. I spent ten years there and she kept my sister and brother. I must have been about seven or eight years old.
>
> My first job at La Purísima was tanning hides for the cots they were building to show where the padres slept. I didn't like it. We had to skin them and let them dry to make the furniture. There were lots of flies and I took about three days of it and that was enough. I went to the Captain and told him I was interested in agriculture and wanted to work in the nursery. He set me up with an interview with Mr. Rowe. I talked to him and took a liking to him and they put me in the nursery. I spent the rest of my time there in the nursery.[23]

Nineteen-year-old Seymour Adler enrolled in the CCC from Los Angeles in 1941, and watched an increase in militarization before he was discharged on September 30, a few months before the Japanese attack at Pearl Harbor.[24]

> When we went home on the weekends, we used to have to compete with the soldiers hitchhiking for rides to Los Angeles. When my enrollment time was getting near the end, they wanted me to re-enroll so they could send me to Alaska and work on the Alaska Highway. But to work there, you had to re-enroll for a year instead of six months. I would have gone, but I had a job offer in Los Angeles. The Flying Tigers came into camp and asked some of the men if they wanted to sign up in the Air Corps. Also, they changed our uniform. Our uniforms were khaki like the Army's and they changed them to a spruce green so we would look different. It didn't last long, because the war broke out and the CCC camps were abandoned.
>
> When I got discharged from the CCC, Mr. Smith, the superintendent, helped me to take the Los Angeles County horticulturist exam and get on the hiring list. And I got hired and worked with them for thirty-four years. I worked with all kinds of plants used in the county parks there, but when

I worked with Mr. Rowe, it was only native varieties. We had the California pear, the rose bushes, hollyhocks, pepper trees, and so on. We went out and collected Monterey Pine cones and baked them to make them pop open and get the seeds out. Mr. Rowe told us to put them in a flat to propagate them, but we tried eating some of them. He laughed at us and said, "Those were to be planted."

I maintained the garden grounds, and on weekends I was the only one that was allowed on the mission grounds to give tours. Mr. Rowe picked me for that because I knew the whole mission. He taught me everything and he didn't want the other enrollees out there collecting money and charging people for tours. All kinds of people just dropped in and I gave them the full tour on weekends. Mr. Rowe made me supervisor of the nursery. I collected seed with him and potted the plants and took care of the garden. The mission roses were big and beautiful and people would come by and want cuttings of them. So we used to give them cuttings for them to propagate. They were called cabbage roses, and they smelled real nice.

In fact, Mr. Rowe has a lilac named after him. *Ceanothus rodianthus.* We had a big potting table where we used to mix the soil. Mr. Rowe would come over and check it as we put sand and different types of material in it to make the right texture for the wild plants. It took about two hours, then we would start potting. When I told Mr. Rowe I wanted some help with a project, he would get me two or three men to help out. Everything was in small pots and then transplanted into gallon cans before we put them out in the garden.

Lompoc was the seed capital of the world then, and I used to walk into town for a drink or a movie and I would get to talk to the growers. Mr. Rowe was very knowledgeable about the plants and taught me a lot. He tried to get me a job with the state, but I got the job with the County of Los Angeles instead. Plants became my whole life.[25]

Adler also became a barracks leader with a variety of responsibilities.

When I came, the barracks leader was leaving my barracks. So after a while, I just took over and the Captain went along with it. When the Captain came in, I had to tell the men to stand at attention at the foot of their beds, and I had to check to see that the barracks was clean and everything was taken care of and things like that. You had your good and bad, and I always tried to make friends with people. I tried to get along with everybody. I tried to learn the Spanish language, and swore with them. I got to be friends with the camp cook, and I used to go into the kitchen all the time and eat chocolate cake.

I was the only Jewish boy in the camp. One time the Captain asked me to say grace and everyone looked at me since I was Jewish. I went along with it. I said, "God bless this food that's placed before us. Amen." I left Jesus Christ out, but everyone just said, "Let's eat." The Captain was real great about it.

Mr. Rowe was just like a father to me. He was tall and distinguished, up in his late fifties when I worked with him. Mr. Smith was great, too. He used to come to the nursery practically every day and ask me how I was doing and how I liked my work. I never even had to do fire duty. Because of the support and responsibility I learned in the CCCs, I could handle working with people in the L.A. county parks. I supervised juveniles on court work orders. Boys on probation got assigned to me and went out on different jobs with me. I worked with lots of boys over that period of thirty-four years.[26]

1. *Santa Barbara News-Press,* September 7, 1937.

2. Ibid.

3. Ibid.

4. "Pearl Chase Papers," Boxes 1-9: La Purísima Mission, *Community Development and Conservation Collection,* Department of Special Collections, Library, University of California at Santa Barbara, California.

5. Frederick C. Hageman and Olaf T. Hagen, *Mission La Purísima Concepción—A Glance Through its History and the Story of its Restoration,* National Park Service, United States Department of the Interior (undated), Mission La Purísima Archives, Lompoc, California, p. 24.

6. Ibid.

7. Ibid.

8. Ibid.; Civilian Conservation Corps, Los Angeles District, *News-Courier,* semi-monthly newspaper, Van Nuys, California, July 15, 1936.

9. National Park Service Press Release, San Francisco Regional Office, July 22, 1937, Landscaping Files, Mission La Purísima Archives, Lompoc, California.

10. Ibid.

11. *News-Courier,* April 1, 1938.

12. *News-Courier,* October 1, 1937.

13. Hageman and Hagen, loc. cit.

14. Ibid.

15. Edith Buckland Webb, *La Purísima Garden* (1957), p. 2, Landscaping Files, Mission La Purísima Archives, Lompoc, California.

16. Edwin Denys Rowe, "The History of a Garden," *Golden Gardens,* California Garden Clubs, June-July 1941, p. 17.
17. Edward Negus Interview with Christine E. Savage, Lompoc, California, July 19, 1989.
18. Ibid.
19. Ibid.
20. *News-Courier,* May 1, 1938.
21. Landscape Maintenance Personnel File, 1937, Landscaping Files, Mission La Purísima Archives, Lompoc, California.
22. Robert Zaragoza Interview with Christine E. Savage, Los Angeles, California, July 24, 1989.
23. Seymour Adler Interview with Christine E. Savage, Alhambra, California, July 25, 1989.
24. Ibid.
25. Ibid.
26. Ibid.

12. Other Mission Buildings

Church and Cemetery

By the spring of 1937, the residence building was well along toward completion, so most of the workmen were moved to the site of the church and cemetery, where work began on April 12.[1] The padres' Annual Report for 1818 had only this to say under the heading "Church":

> One of forked posts having collapsed, a temporary church of adobe was built on the same site, with a tiled roof, loft, sacristy, and counter sacristy.

The information regarding the cemetery and bell tower was even less illuminating. The statement in the Annual Report for 1821, under the heading "Church," reads: "There has been placed close to this a cemetery with belfry, all new."[2] Hageman solved this problem by using the "point of view" perspective of the photographer with a photo dated circa 1880, which he obtained from the McCurry Photo Service in Sacramento.[3]

> Only one photograph showing a small fragment of the ruined church could be found, and it was taken from a location on the hill on the east side of the valley and included the residence building also. From an enlargement of this one photograph, by making a transparency on a piece of glass and with it locating the camera point, it was possible to work out the dimensions of the building and the heights of the doors and windows. The building was 174 feet, 3 inches long; 46 feet, 4 inches wide, including the covered corridor along the west side which was 12 feet, 7 inches wide, and 26 feet high. The nave, including the sanctuary, was 144 feet, 4 inches long, and 24 feet, 8 inches wide; and the ceiling height was 19 feet above the floor of the nave. The entire floor of the nave was paved with 10 x 10 x 2 inch tile and the sanctuary floor was of redwood. The plastered walls were 4 feet, 4 inches thick.[4] On May 14, 1937, Father Coffee, delegate

general of the Franciscan Order in Rome, came to La Purísima to lay the cornerstone of the church in a simple ceremony.[5]

During the excavation of the sanctuary, the grave of Padre Mariano Payeras was carefully uncovered and the skeleton was measured and photographed. A masonry vault, capped with a concrete slab, was then built around it and the grave again covered over with earth. The position of this grave furnished the only clue to the location of the pulpit, as no information whatever could be gathered from the ruined walls or floor.[6]

The cemetery, measuring 134 feet, 4 inches long by 56 feet, 9 inches wide, was enclosed by a plastered adobe wall three feet thick. As no data could be found regarding the height, capping, and door openings to these walls, the details were copied largely from old photographs of the original walls at Mission San Antonio de Padua. They are 8 feet, 4 inches high and are capped with two double rows of roof tiles, a single longitudinal row of tile forming a ridge. Some of the original tiles for the cemetery walls were found in the ruins and they proved to be somewhat smaller than the roof tiles from the buildings. The new tiles are exact duplicates of the originals. An arched opening fitted with double doors, in the south wall, provides an entrance for funeral processions.[7]

Campañario

No photographs or documentary evidence was found which furnished any data concerning the bell tower, or campañario. Evidence of the horizontal measurements and the structural materials was furnished by the original, massive foundation, which was still intact, but Hageman borrowed the design largely from the original bell tower at Mission Santa Ines, which had been documented with some excellent photographs.[8] The La Purísima campañario was built to measure 20 feet, 10 inches long by 8 feet, 10 inches wide at the base, and is 33 feet high, exclusive of the four-foot wooden cross on its crest. It is a pierced opening design with openings for three bells, two of which are on the same level, with the third one above. It was attached to the south end of the church and access to the bell ringing platform was by means of a wooden staircase from the cemetery. Fragments of the original plaster, found at the site, indicated that plastered walls of the tower were not white-washed like the other buildings, but were a light pink, as were the cemetery walls. This color was reproduced with native pigment when the new structures were plastered.[9] Included in the material lists for construction of the church, campañario and cemetery walls were 50,000 adobe bricks, 20,000 roof tiles, and 18,000 floor tiles.[10]

Constructing the campañario (1937). Note the adobe bricks, which are still un-plastered. [MISSION LA PURISIMA ARCHIVES]

After the missions were secularized in 1834, many of La Purísima's furnishings were removed to other missions and parish churches by the padres to prevent their theft and despoilation by vandals.[11] One of La Purísima's 1817 campañario bells, forged in Lima, Peru, hung in the belfry of the Roman Catholic church in the nearby town of Guadalupe until 1941 when Vee Smith brought it back to La Purísima with the Church's permission. In a letter to Hageman he wrote, "You can imagine our elation on getting the Guadalupe bell. I think one of the most thrilling experiences of my varied career was that of climbing up into the Guadalupe tower and lowering that bell."[12]

Shops and Quarters Building

Construction of the shops and quarters building, which stood between the residence building and the church, began on April 11, 1938.[13] The padres' Annual Report for 1816 described this building as follows:

There has been constructed a building 100 varas in length with 6 varas clear width, walls of one adobe thick, roof of tile and corridors on both sides. Its purpose is for the guardroom, dwellings for the troops, for the mayordomos, a carpenter shop and for the new looms.

This building had suffered more deterioration than the residence or church. Hageman explained to the Advisory Committee how he drew plans for the reconstructed shops and quarters building.

There were no other data available, other than what could be gathered from the original foundations and the debris covering them. The general design of the elevations and structural details, therefore, had to be more or less conjectural and are a composite resulting from studies of photographs of similar buildings, notably those of Missions San Fernando, San Antonio and San Juan Bautista, and from the adjoining buildings at La Purísima. All data used as a basis for the design of this building were clearly and convincingly reviewed in the folio of supporting data submitted with the plans.[14]

The building was L-shaped. The main portion measured 323 feet, 8 inches in length, and the wing, at a right angle to the main portion at the south end, extended 56 feet to the west, almost touching the church. This wing formed the south wall of a huge rectangular enclosure which extended the full length of the building. The enclosure was divided by a partition wall into two patios, one measuring 175 feet in length, the other 124 feet. The outside width of the building was 22 feet, except for the covered east and west corridors, which were 8 feet, 4 inches and 9 feet, 11 inches, respectively, making an overall width of 40 feet, 3 inches. It contained a single row of 17 rooms, and the walls were 30 inches thick. As reconstructed, the building is just short of 20 feet high.[15]

The roof construction of this building was different from that of the others because there were no ceilings or subroof. The roof tiles were placed on spaced redwood strips fastened to the rafters, so that the entire roof structure was exposed to view from the rooms and corridors. The ridge beam was supported by the gabled adobe partitions, but in the longer rooms additional support was given to the ridge by notched posts resting on bolsters lashed with rawhide to the tops of massive beams. These spanned the rooms and projected through the walls to the outside.[16] Leo Mandeville had a specific recollection of how those rawhide strips were made.

They used the lavanderia to soak the cowhides. I remember it was full of wet cowhides that they were soaking to soften them up so they could cut them into strips to tie the beams together.[17]

The material lists for this building, including the patio walls, indicate that 90,000 adobe bricks, 34,000 roof tiles, and 12,000 floor tiles were required for its construction.[18] The patio walls are 2 feet thick and 7 feet high, plastered and capped with two opposing single rows of roof tiles topped by a single, longitudinal row of tiles.[19] A single door through the partition wall permits passing from one patio to the other.

Hageman described the excavation discoveries in the patio.

In the larger, south patio were discovered the foundation of a large, outdoor oven and the bases of several fireplaces, undoubtedly where cooking was done. In the other patio three column foundations were found, with the remains of adobe columns, which seem to have supported the roof of an open shelter, one of which rested on the dividing wall of the patios. In this patio there was also found a small pit, lined with floor tile set on edge, which was possibly used for soaking the clay used to manufacture clay ollas [large, bulging widemouthed earthenware jars with looped handles] and other vessels.[20]

It seemed to Hageman from this and other evidence that the rooms bordering the larger patio were the living quarters, guardroom, and jail, while the rooms bordering the smaller patio were the workshops. Hageman also deduced that the large room at the southeast corner facing on the open plaza in front of the church was the guardroom.[21] He envisioned what it had looked like 120 years before his time.

From a tall staff in the plaza in front of the Guardroom once fluttered the flag of Spain, only to be replaced shortly by the green, white, and red banner of the newly formed Republica de Mexico. In front of the church and beside the shops and quarters building is the hard, bare plaza where the padres assembled the Indians and instructed them in the orders of the day.[22]

---

1. Frederick C. Hageman and Olaf T. Hagen, *Mission La Purísima Concepción—A Glance Through its History and the Story of its Restoration,* National Park Service, United States Department of the Interior (undated), Mission La Purísima Archives, Lompoc, California, p. 26.

2. Ibid.
3. H.W. Whitsitt letter to Southern Pacific Railroad Company, September 20, 1935, correspondence files, Mission La Purísima Archives, Lompoc, California.
4. Hageman and Hagen, loc. cit.
5. Fred Hageman letter to Cora Older, March 31, 1938, correspondence files, Mission La Purísima Archives, Lompoc, California.
6. Hageman and Hagen, op. cit., p. 27.
7. Hageman and Hagen, op. cit., p. 28.
8. Hageman and Hagen, op. cit., p. 27.
9. Ibid.
10. Hageman and Hagen, op. cit., p. 28.
11. Marie T. Walsh, *The Mission Bells of California,* Harr Wagner Publishing Company (San Francisco, 1934), p. 87.
12. H.V. Smith letter to Fred Hageman, February 4, 1941, correspondence files, Mission La Purísima Archives, Lompoc, California.
13. Hageman and Hagen, op. cit., p. 28.
14. Hageman and Hagen, op. cit., p. 29.
15. Ibid.
16. Hageman and Hagen, op. cit., p. 30.
17. Leo E. Mandeville Interview with Christine E. Savage, Santa Barbara, California, July 17, 1989.
18. Hageman and Hagen, op. cit., p. 30.
19. Ibid.
20. Ibid.
21. Ibid.
22. Hagemen and Hagen, op. cit., p. 31.

13. Camp Recreation

The Boxing Ring

While the Santa Rosa Camp was still in tents in front of the mission ruins, an informal boxing area had been set up by the company commander as part of the regular exercise program for enrollees. As soon as Company 1951 moved up on the mesa behind the mission, the Army set up a fully-equipped camp boxing ring behind the mess hall.[1] Throughout the country, each camp had been issued a variety of sporting equipment: baseball gloves, balls, bats, horseshoes, and boxing gloves and protective headgear.[2] Captain Tornell was a boxing enthusiast and worked out with a punching bag each morning before his first cup of coffee.[3] He usually served as referee at La Purísima's boxing ring, whether the match was to settle a barracks fight or merely a contest between two talented camp boxers.[4] Some enrollees from Los Angeles like Ray Ellis had actually fought professionally, and could handle themselves with great skill.[5]

Boxing became the main sport in camp because the sporadically organized baseball and football teams were consistently beaten by other CCC camps—perhaps due to the lack of adequate coaching and the changes in enrollment every six months. For a brief period in the autumn of 1936, hopes ran high for the Mission Builders football team, when an especially brawny group of enrollees were transferred to La Purísima from disbanded CCC Camp Steckel Park. But they were beaten 13-2 by their own twin camp—The Lompoc Clodhoppers—on the hill behind the mission.[6] Boxing prevailed as the sport of choice for both participants and observers at La Purísima. Gilbert Ballesterose particularly remembered a bantam-weight boxer from East Los Angeles named "Tiny" Martinez who was the pride of the camp's ring.[7] Seymour Adler remembered running along with another camp boxer, Chuckie Garcia, for three or four miles in the evening three times a week so Garcia wouldn't break training while enrolled in the CCC.[8]

The Barracks Poker Game

It was one of those things that they weren't supposed to do, but everyone did anyway. Almost every barracks had its own game, and often the barracks leaders would join in. Enrollees even suspected that the company commander had a game going with the staff sergeant and the mess sergeant.[9] Poker was one of the mainstays of recreation in the camp, even though it does not appear in any official records. The CCC men played for small stakes with the $5 they received each month on payday. (The government automatically deducted $25 from their dollar-a-day wages to mail home a U.S. Treasury check to the enrollee's parents.) Enrollees commonly spent their $5 on cigarettes at the camp canteen and on poker in the barracks. Many stayed perpetually in debt from one payday to another and bummed cigarettes and cash from their friends. Ray "Joker" Ellis elaborated.

> I ran the game only for the guys in my barracks and they stayed quiet about it. It was an orderly game and I didn't let them lose more than they could afford to lose. If I saw that they were getting over their head, they had to shove off. It was a fun game and I took ten percent of the pot to furnish the cigarettes, cards, and change. I liked to play cards.
>
> I always sent my poker money home so it wouldn't get stolen. Before sending it home, I always slept with the bills in my bunk, in the mattress. But it took a lot of change to run the game and I kept that in a coffee can in my locker. One night, the company commander raided the barracks right after a game. They were looking for something that had been stolen, not to bust up the game. They looked in my locker and asked me where I got all that change and, naturally, I couldn't say I had it for the poker game. I told them I saved coins, and they swallowed it. The sergeant gave me a little rhubarb about it, but what could they say? I told them I saved coins. I had four or five cartons of cigarettes in my locker, too, and I didn't smoke. But they didn't know that.[10]

Liquor

Alcoholic beverages were forbidden in camp, so those men who were old enough to drink had to walk into Lompoc when they felt like having a beer. Occasionally, a man would feel that camp life was getting a little dull, and sneak liquor into the barracks. An enrollee in Frank Hines' barracks got acquainted with a Lompoc farmer who sold him some home-made wine.

He would make a run down the hill behind camp to the farm and come back with a couple of gallons. It was green wine, not completely aged. But we didn't care and drank it anyway. It gave me one of the worst hangovers I've ever had in my life. The next morning, I had to go down and plaster that damn building in the hot sun with that adobe flying in my face and getting sick to my stomach. The foreman was mad at me because I'd have to take off every five minutes to be sick. Superintendent Smith walked by and saw I was hung over and asked, "If you can't hold your liquor, why do you drink?" I said, "Sir, nobody could hold that liquor!"[11]

Hines remembered another enrollee from Tennessee whose father was a moonshiner.

He got leave to go back and visit his family, and when he came back, he had a load of "white mule" with him—good old Tennessee corn liquor. Oh, that was good whiskey! The best I've ever tasted—smooth. We kept it hidden and sipped a little every now and then. It was a sad day when it was gone. He had brought the bottles back in his barracks bag. I don't think he even had any clothes in there when he came back to camp![12]

Hazing

Good-natured harassment of new men was a common practice in all CCC camps. Enrollees at La Purísima usually did not persecute newcomers much after the first week of short-sheeting, sand in the blankets, and moving a sleeping man's cot outside. Still, everyone was subject at all times to the bucket of water propped up on a partially open door.[13] Enrollees looked upon these forms of hazing as a way of singling out men who would not endure camp life, "the ones who couldn't take it." Playful wrestling in the barracks was common. There were occasional forced scrubbing parties with soap and stiff Army brushes for those new men who chose not to shower daily and offended their barracks mates, but those men were warned first. All newcomers got the worst jobs at the work site during their first week, usually in the mudpits or plastering. Zaragoza remembered some horseplay near the mission job site.

I was wrestling with a guy one day. We were just playing around, but he got a hold around my neck like a lock on there. All I can remember is that I just wasn't there any more. I went blank. And when I woke up, he was over me hitting me in the face to bring me back. And he was so scared he was white as a ghost. When he got that lock on, the more I struggled, the harder he held on until he choked me.[14]

Captain Tornell's Garden

The LEM nightwatchman at the Twin Camps was also a beekeeper, and Captain Tornell allowed him to keep beehives at the north end of the CCC mesa. He produced honey for the camp's kitchen, and the bees made use of Captain Tornell's flower garden around the camp administration building. Tornell took great pride in the little garden because it was the only bit of color on the bare parade ground. He placed protective rocks around it so no one would walk through the flowers.[15] One sunny summer afternoon, Frank Hines was walking by the administration building.

> I became aware of this humming all around me and I suddenly realized I was right in the middle of a swarm of bees. Without even thinking, I took off as though I were jet propelled right through the captain's flower garden with my big size-twelve CCC shoes making huge footprints among the flowers. There was no doubt that somebody had run right through Tornell's flower garden, but nobody saw me do it and I wasn't about to confess to it either. But they had quite an investigation trying to find out who had trampled the flowers. They were sure it was done on purpose.[16]

CCC Education at La Purísima

Despite the fact that many men nationwide learned to read and write, earned their high school diplomas, and received some vocational training while in the CCC, most enrollees ignored these opportunities. Because the educational offerings in each camp were always optional, the majority of enrollees chose recreational activities during their leisure time. A dedicated group of LEMs, mostly unemployed teachers, worked as camp education advisers all across the nation, but they were unable to offer both academic and vocational classes for hundreds of enrollees, and work as individual career counselors at the same time. Also, they received little cooperation from the Army and Technical Services personnel because they felt their primary goal was the work project.[17]

La Purísima Camp was no exception. There were 409 men enrolled in the Twin Camps in 1940, and many of these had not yet graduated from high school. Only three chose to take classes in camp to obtain their high school diplomas that year.[18] Frank Hines described what they were up against.

> There was not too much cooperation between the camp educator and the Army and NPS supervisors. They were competing for enrollees' time. The NPS supervisors would get upset if we were held on the parade ground in

the morning for special announcements that made us late for the work. But we enrollees didn't suffer—we laughed at both of them.

As my enrollment time at La Purísima was drawing to a close, the camp educational adviser, John C. Gambell, told me he could set up a class schedule so I could complete my high school education. I needed to re-enroll and complete a year and a half of high school in six months. I had to stop working on the mission and become part of the crew shifts in the kitchen. There were two full crews cooking for the Twin Camps, who each worked three days on and three days off. This allowed me enough time off to study and take exams. The mess sergeant, Scotty, put me on kitchen duty. Each crew worked three fifteen-hour days and then had three days off, so the cooking was alternated. On each crew there were four cooks and four KPs on the shift. I started earning educational credit toward my high school diploma on this schedule. It was a killer, but I made it.

When the two other men and I completed our high school educations, we were heroes. They had a big to-do out on the parade grounds and Captain Tornell read off our names and everybody cheered. My classes were English Grammar I and II, Journalism, Psychology, Government, and Surveying. I was also given high school credit for the work I was doing. Mr. Gambell gave me all the exams and arranged all the study periods. The courses had been set up by the State Education Department, and there were no individual teachers.

Mr. Gamble was an employee of the CCC, not the Lompoc School District. He was supportive of anyone who wanted to continue their education. There were so few of us who were really trying that he seemed like a father to us. He was there all the time when we needed him. Although some of the boys wanted to learn real trades that they could use when they got out, most of the rest of the enrollees couldn't see any point in trying for it during their six-month enrollment period.[19]

Morning safety classes for all crews at the Twin Camps began on October 1, 1938. These were often the only times when some enrollees were in a formal instructional setting. Seymour Adler took a few evening classes, mostly first aid and history, but did not value those classes over the trade he was learning in the mission's garden. "What did I need that for? I wanted to get into something I liked, which was horticulture."[20] Harry Davis remembered taking an auto mechanics course that tied in with his job as a camp truck driver, but he took no academic offerings because he already had his high school diploma.[21]

'IILIAN CONSERVATION CORPS
OFFICE OF THE DIRECTOR
WASHINGTON, D. C.

Date   February 19, 1941

CCC CAMP EDUCATIONAL REPORT

Camp No. SP-29   Company No. 1951   Post Office   Lompoc   State   California
   SCS-9   2950

(Subjects of Instruction:)

Auto Mechanics	English	Radio Communication	U. S. History
Band-Orchestra	Glee Club	Reading	Vehicle Operation
Blue Print Reading	Journalism	Salesmanship	Welding
Business Training	Penmanship	Slide Rule	
Carpentry	Photography	Trade Mathematics	
Civics	Printing	Typing	

RELATED EDUCATIONAL WORK
Lectures, Visual Education, Job Training, First Aid, Safety Education, Etc.

Two (2) Chaplain's lectures each month. Two (2) Co. 1951 SP-29 safety lectures and two (2) Co. 2950 SCS-9 safety lectures monthly. Weekly showing of educational films from HMCA film library. Seven (7) sections of First Aid classes meet one (1) to three (3) times weekly. On the job training as follows: By Technical Service Personnel SP-29:- Restoration of Mission Buildings; Adobe Building Construction; Road Construction; Nursery and Plant Propagation; Concrete Construction; Making and (over

OTHER FACILITIES
Libraries, Size, Active, or Inactive, Newspapers, Etc.

Library 22' by 40', 2050 fiction, 1080 non-fiction, 187 enrollees read 423 books in January. Five (5) daily newspapers. Twenty-three (23) magazine subscriptions: fifteen (15) monthly, two (2) bi-monthly, six (6) weekly. Average daily attendance in library:- 101 enrollees. Feature length 16 mm sound film shown weekly in camp theatre on All Camp Night (Wednesday).

SCOPE OF INSTRUCTION
Grade of Work and How Conducted

Evening Classes chiefly vocational. Cooperating high school furnishes eight (8) evening high school teachers; WPA furnishes three (3) teachers in Adult Education Program (California State Department of Education). Elementary subjects and academic subjects given as necessary to qualify enrollees for elementary and high school graduation.

Is Educational Adviser assigned to Camp? Yes. Do Camp Officers conduct courses? Yes.
Do members of Technical Personnel conduct courses? Yes.
Specify number of nights each week devoted to education? Four (4)
Present company strength (184) 1951 Average attendance daily (157) Co 1951 SP-29
(186) 2950 (not general assembly) (86) Co 2950 SCS-9

RESULTS OF EDUCATIONAL WORK

Signed   JOHN C. GAMBLL
Camp Educational Adviser   69790

For Remarks use other side of sheet.

```
RELATED EDUCATIONAL WORK (Continued)

laying roof tile, Floor Tile, and adobe bricks; Furniture Making; Truck Driving;
Blacksmithing; Records and Reports; Moving Trees by boxing and balling/
By Technical Service Personnel SCS-9;- Dam Construction, Concrete Construction;
Masonry Construction; Surveying; Drafting; Tree Planting; Vegetative Lined Ditches;
Pasture Planting; Terracing; Revetments; Contour Ditches; Fences; Records and
Reports; Warehouse and Inventory; Tractor and Bulldozer Operation; Truck Driving;
Auto Mechanics./
By Administrative Personnel:- Cooking, Baking; Clerical; Barbering; Laundry; Supply.
Leisure-Time Job Training: SP-29:-Given at the job after work hours one-half (½)
hour weekly/  SCS-9:-Given in morning classes, one-half (½) hour daily by crews
(morning classes temporarily suspended, to be resumed March 3, 1941).
```

Many years later sixty-nine-year-old Robert Zaragoza remembered why he never took the optional academic classes and few of the vocational offerings.

> I was only eighteen years old, and I needed three years to finish high school. That seemed like a lifetime to me then. I never knew I was going to get this old![22]

The Army managed the educational program in each CCC camp and it chose to rotate both the educational advisers and military commanders frequently. Personnel turnover continued at La Purísima as F.A. Morrison took over from Peter Quin as educational adviser on May 1, 1936, serving until November 1936, when he resigned.[23] Willard T. Day then assumed direction of the educational work of Company 1951, together with his duties as educational adviser of Lompoc Camp's Company 2950 at the same site.[24] Day continued to act as adviser for Company 1951 until August 26, 1937, when Jospeh W. Winn took over as educational director.[25]

On February 1, 1937, Captain Carroll D. Hudson was given command of La Purísima Camp.[26] In May 1938, Company 1951 was further united with Company 2950 when Captain Claus A. Tornell was appointed as the single coordinating Army officer for the Twin Camps.[27] The two companies used the same mess hall and recreation hall. The building formerly used as the recreation hall for Company 1951 was converted into a Twin Camps theater. The mess hall formerly used by

Company 2950 was remodeled and designated the educational building for the Twin Camps. The educational programs for the two companies were combined, and a branch of Lompoc Union High School was established at the camp.[28]

Captain Hudson returned to private employment when his tour of duty with the CCC was completed, and Captain William P. Robinson was assigned to his position as commander of the La Purísima Camp and assistant to Captain Tornell on January 20, 1938.[29] On November 5, 1938, Dr. Albert H. Satterlee was commissioned as a first lieutenant in the Medical Corps Reserve of the U.S. Army, and assigned to the Lompoc Camp, where he served both companies.[30]

The Santa Rosa Camp educational adviser asked Negus to lecture on construction techniques in the evenings, but Negus refused because he had already been performing those techniques on the job with the enrollees all day long. He felt the educators interrupted the work project. "I got disgusted with them," he said.[31]

One of the other educational staff members at La Purísima Camp was Ernest H. Brooks who offered photography classes in the evenings.[32] A darkroom had been set up in the camp, and the enrollees purchased their own cameras, paper, and developing fluid. Both Zaragoza and Davis remembered learning photo developing there.[33] Davis even sold some of his better prints for a nickel each. The agricultural Lompoc Valley was famous as a source of flower seeds, and colorful blankets of flower fields were common in the area. Ernest Brooks had a photography studio in Lompoc and had earned a wide-ranging reputation as a flower photographer.[34] Leo Mandeville also took Brooks' photography classes at La Purísima, and remembered a shoot where " . . . one Sunday Mr. Brooks had a couple of models and a very fancy automobile in front of the reconstructed mission and we were taking pictures of it for class."[35]

Brooks founded the Brooks Institute of Photography in Santa Barbara in 1945, just as professional color photography was becoming popular. The Institute has since become internationally famous as a school for the training of professional photographers, and its success has been based partly on the instructional skills Brooks acquired with his CCC students at the Twin Camps.

The Blue Banner

In November-December 1937, and in February-March 1938, Lompoc Company 2950 earned the Blue Banner, the highest camp evaluation rating in the Los Angeles CCC District.[36] During January 1937, Camp Lompoc had originated the "Lompoc Plan of Orientation" for training new enrollees during a two-week period. This plan came to be used by all Soil Conservation Service camps in Region Nine.[37]

The Twin Camps' flag pole, which held the Blue Banner in 1938.
[MISSION LA PURISIMA ARCHIVES]

In April 1938, just before the administrative combination of Companies 1951 and 2950 into the Twin Camps, the two camps received their last individual camp evaluations, and placed first and second in the District.[38] The Los Angeles CCC District provided special banners to be displayed from the company flagpole of each camp that earned consistently high ratings. For one month—April 1938— Twin Camps had the distinction of flying two pennants for first and second place below the national flag.

The feeling of pride in their camp and respect for their supervisors was evident among the men in more ways than the Blue Banner revealed. On February 1, 1939, La Purísima's head baker and baking instructor, Henry Koenig, died in the

Photo taken for Twin Camps Yearbook (1940) by Ernest H. Brooks
[MISSION LA PURISIMA ARCHIVES]

Santa Maria hospital.[39] Koenig was a veteran of the German army of World War I, where he suffered the loss of one lung. The *News-Courier* reported, "He left no estate and no relatives in California. He was alone, except for a few scattered friends and 400 enrollees at the Twin Camps—but that was enough." Enrollees contributed pocket change totaling $55 to keep Koenig out of a pauper's grave and to give him a proper funeral.[40] During its final year of reconstruction work, the La Purísima CCC Camp was commanded by Captain Raymond C. Ball, who took over for Captain Tornell when he was transferred to the Boulder City CCC Camp near Las Vegas, Nevada, in December 1939.[41] Ball's assistants were Captain Dennis M. Murphy and Captain Linton S. Black, all regular Army.[42]

1. *Voice of the Twin Camps,* La Purísima CCC Camp Lompoc, California, December 6, 1935.
2. Civilian Conservation Corps Headquarters, Ninth Corps Area, *CCC Instructions* (San Francisco Presidio, July 1, 1938), p. 232; Albert W. Jernberg, *My Brush Monkeys—A Narrative of the CCC,* Richard R. Smith Publishers (New York, 1941).
3. Franklin E. Hines Interview with Christine E. Savage, Los Angeles, California, July 21, 1989.
4. Raymond E. Ellis, Sr., Interview with Christine E. Savage, Santa Barbara, California, July 27, 1989.
5. M. Gilbert Ballesterose Interview with Christine E. Savage, Buellton, California, July 26, 1989.
6. Civilian Conservation Corps, Los Angeles District, *News-Courier,* semi-monthly newspaper, Van Nuys, California, December 15, 1936.
7. Ballesterose Interview.
8. Seymour Adler Interview with Christine E. Savage, Alhambra, California, July 25, 1989.
9. Robert Zaragoza Interview with Christine E. Savage, Los Angeles, California, July 24, 1989; Hines Interview.
10. Ellis Interview.
11. Hines Interview.
12. Ibid.
13. Hines Interview; Ellis Interview; Ballesterose Interview; Zaragosa Interview.
14. Zaragoza Interview.
15. Hines Interview.
16. Ibid.
17. Edward Negus Interview with Christine E. Savage, Lompoc, California, July 19, 1989; Albert W. Jernberg, *My Brush Monkeys—A Narrative of the CCC,* Richard R. Smith Publishers (New York, 1941).
18. Hines Interview.
19. Ibid.
20. Adler Interview.
21. Harry A. Davis Interview with Christine E. Savage, Claremont, California, July 22, 1989.
22. Zaragoza Interview.

23. Civilian Conservation Corps, Los Angeles District, *Official Annual,* Ninth Corps Area (Van Nuys, California, 1938), p. 119.
24. Ibid.
25. Ibid.
26. Ibid.
27. CCC *Annual,* p. 119, *News-Courier,* May 15, 1938.
28. CCC *Annual,* p. 119.
29. Ibid.
30. Ibid.
31. Negus Interview.
32. Leo E. Mandeville Interview with Christine E. Savage, Santa Barbara, California, July 17, 1989.
33. Zaragoza Interview; Davis Interview.
34. *News-Courier,* July 15, 1936.
35. Mandeville Interview.
36. CCC *Annual,* p. 119.
37. Ibid.
38. CCC *Annual,* p. 119; *News-Courier,* April 15, 1938.
39. *News-Courier,* February 15, 1939.
40. Ibid.
41. *News-Courier,* December 15, 1939.
42. Ibid.

14. Final Work

Hageman Relieved

In February 1937, Howard V. Smith, called Vee by his friends, arrived to relieve Hageman as La Purísima's project superintendent[1] Hageman was to give more time and attention to the architectural and historical research work necessary to insure a true reconstruction of the mission, and he was given an assistant architect from the National Park Service, Harvey R. Harwood, in 1938.[2] Ed Negus described the turnover.

> The job of project superintendent was just a lot of office paper work and Vee Smith was an outstanding superintendent of CCC camps. He came from Brand Park Camp in the Glendale area. Our district inspector, Phil Primm, told us we were going to have a darn good superintendent in Vee Smith, and he was. He was outstanding.[3]

Fifteen years after his appointment at La Purísima, Smith wrote a fond remembrance of his days at the mission to Newton Drury, chief of the California Division of Parks (and subsequent director of the National Park Service).

> I worked there for nearly six years and had an unforgettable experience. It was one of those experiences which, I suppose, comes to each man once in a lifetime and overshadows everything else. Hageman set a new standard for this type of work which has been a model for so many restorations that have been started since. I have never ceased to give La Purísima much thought.[4]

However, some supervisory positions at La Purísima Camp had no turnover: Edwin Denys Rowe remained as landscape foreman; Walt Stewart continued to supervise all carpentry in the woodshop; Ed Negus remained as construction foreman; Ralph E. Ames continued to oversee the brick and tile making operations; and William Cassuth stayed on as mechanic and motor pool foreman.

On August 1, 1938, George Morrison was appointed project superintendent of the Lompoc Soil Conservation Service Camp, Company 2950, replacing engineer

Arthur Darsey, who was transferred to Palos Verdes Camp. Also in 1938, First Lieutenant Claus Tornell was promoted to captain.[5]

WPA Artists

While the Civilian Conservation Corps provided jobs for unskilled working men, another New Deal program, the Works Progress Administration (WPA), functioned similarly for trained professionals. Teachers, nurses, actors, artists, and musicians were also out of work during the Depression. During November and

WPA artist painting pulpit in the chapel of the residence building (1938).
[MISSION LA PURISIMA ARCHIVES]

Final Work

Two enrollees painting church interior (1938). [MISSION LA PURISIMA ARCHIVES]

December 1940, an artist from the Index of American Design came to La Purísima to decorate the interior of the reconstructed church.[6] Unemployed painter Harry Helmle was paid $25.00 per month plus expenses through WPA funds, and was supervised by Mr. Dana Bartlett of the Index's office in Los Angeles.[7]

Helmle had previously painted a number of murals in public buildings in and around Los Angeles.[8] Bartlett's department had worked out most of the original La Purísima decorations from the old plaster fragments[9] and from the research files of the Index of American Design,[10] and Helmle painted the walls of the church, the altar decorations, and the pulpit with the assistance of two enrollees.

Bartlett also found a sculptor and wood carver, Harold Gebhardt, who was brought to the mission to work on the statues in the church.[11] The Federal Art Project of Southern California had previously sent artists to decorate the pulpit and chancel rail in the chapel of the padres' residence building under the supervision of Douglas Parshall of Santa Barbara.[12] When the art projects were nearly completed, the Federal Art Project sent Paul Park to photograph the work.[13]

[151]

Old Mission Days

After the State Park Commission acquired more land for the mission site in 1941, park employees' living quarters and support structures were prepared, as the state prepared to take over the full-time maintenance of the complex. Santa Barbara County planned a special celebration for two of its three missions with Old Mission Days, December 4-7, 1941. That weekend was chosen because of its special significance to California mission founding history.[14] The Roman Catholic feast day of Saint Barbara was December 4, and her name was bestowed on Mission Santa Barbara, founded on December 4, 1786. Mission La Purísima had been founded on the feast of the Immaculate Conception, December 8, 1787.

County elites assembled in a special Old Mission Days Planning Committee. With them, other planners and volunteer groups put together a four-day program of receptions, exhibits, religious ceremonies, illustrated talks, tours, sacred concerts, dinners, and fiestas, to be held at the Santa Barbara and La Purísima missions.[15]

Old Mission Days culminated at newly restored La Purísima, of which the county was justly proud. It was the 154th anniversary of the dedication of the first mission at Lompoc, and a religious ceremony was designed to duplicate the original founding dedication ritual conducted by Padre Presidente Lasuén.[16] A plaque donated by the Grand Parlor of the Native Daughters of the Golden West was placed over Padre Payeras's grave and dedicated. A 1771 painting entitled "La Virgin Purísima" by Michel Cabrera, the "Murillo of Mexico," was donated by local adobe buff John Southworth and unveiled in the church. The CCC boys, dressed as Chumash Indians, demonstrated adobe brick making and rode about in a carreta pulled by two oxen.[17] The carreta was the only wheeled vehicle used on El Camino Real, the King's Royal Highway, that connected all of California's Spanish missions.

Visitors brought box lunches and were served coffee, beans, and tortillas under a covered ramada on the mission grounds. Guests of the State Park Commission received special luncheon passes (at sixty cents each) and ate a more substantial meal in the CCC mess hall on the hill behind the mission. Santa Barbara's Franciscan seminary, St. Anthony's, provided a choir to sing authentic mission music, and officials from the State Park Commission gave an illustrated talk on the rebuilding of La Purísima. The mission's bells rang for the first time since 1836.[18]

Hundreds attended, and it was standing room only for the High Mass celebrated by Fr. Augustine Hobrecht, O.F.M., in the reconstructed church.[19] As the

Old Mission Days

In Santa Barbara County

COUNTY COMMITTEE:

General Chairman
CHARLES A. STORKE

Advisory Chairman
MISS PEARL CHASE

Vice-Chairmen
MRS. FRANCIS B. LINN
DR. ANNA McCAUGHEY
JOSEPH McFARLAND
GEORGE W. ORMSBY
RAYMOND ROMERO

Treasurer
WILLIAM GUNTERMANN

Secretary
E. S. CONNER

MR. AND MRS. RONALD M. ADAM
H. L. BLAISDELL
MISS ELIZABETH BUELL
FR. FINNIAN CARROLL, O. F. M., Cap.
ARTHUR COGGESHALL
MISS MICHAELA De La CUESTA
T. WILSON DIBBLEE
MRS. JOHN F. DRENNEN
WILLIAM NORTH DUANE
MRS. MURIEL EDWARDS
DR. WILLIAM H. ELLISON
DON FOLLETT
MRS. HELEN R. FRANCE
EARL P. HANSON
FR. AUGUSTINE HOBRECHT, O. F. M.
MRS A. J. HOLZMAN
MRS. MARGARET HOURIHAN
MRS. HILMAR KOEFOD
FRANK J. McCOY
FR. JAMES McGOVERN
FRANK MIRATTI
JOHN J. MITCHELL
MISS HELEN MURPHY
FRANCIS NOEL
WALLACE PENFIELD
FR. PATRICK RODDY, O. F. M.
E. DENYS ROWE
CLARENCE RUTH
MONROE RUTHERFORD
H. V. SMITH
MR. AND MRS. E. H. STAMM
MR. AND MRS. SAMUEL J. STANWOOD
PAUL SWEETSER
FREDERICK TOLBERT
MRS. M. F. TURNAGE
HUBERT VOIGHT
PAUL WHITNEY
MRS. WALTER ZIESCHE

ORGANIZATIONS COOPERATING:

Santa Barbara County Supervisors
Mayors and Councils of Santa Barbara,
Lompoc and Santa Maria
All-Year Club of Southern California
California Historical Association
Chambers of Commerce of Santa Barbara
County, Lompoc, Santa Maria
and Carpinteria
City and County Education Departments
City and County Libraries
County Federation of Womens Clubs
Daughters of the American Revolution
La Purisima Advisory Committee
La Purisima Mission Association
of Lompoc
Los Rancheros Visitadores
Mission Council of Boy Scouts
Mission Trails Associaton
National Council of Catholic Women
Native Daughters of the Golden West
Native Sons of the Golden West
Plans and Planting Committee
Santa Barbara Junior Chamber
of Commerce
Santa Barbara Museum of Natural
History
Solvang Businessmen's Association

HEADQUARTERS:
COVARRUBIAS ADOBE
715 SANTA BARBARA STREET
SANTA BARBARA, CALIF.
TELEPHONE 22857

November 27, 1941.

       I am enclosing an announcement of Old Mission Days Celebration, a new event in Santa Barbara County, which commemorates the founding of two of our great missions - Santa Barbara and Purisima.

       We are emphasizing the importance of preserving our historic landmarks and the value of the work done by individuals and public agencies to this end.

       We wish you might join in some of the events of the week with us.

Very cordially yours,

Pearl Chase

Pearl Chase, Advisory Chairman
Old Mission Days in Santa Barbara
County.

PC:H

A commemoration of an important period in California History, with the cooperation of the Catholic Church. State Division of Beaches and Parks. National Park Service, Civilian Conservation Corps, and Patriotic and Civic Associations. Missions in Santa Barbara County Founded: Santa Barbara, December 4, 1786; La Purisima Concepcion, December 8, 1787; Santa Ines, September 17, 1804.

PROGRAM--OLD MISSION DAYS IN SANTA BARBARA COUNTY

DAILY—THURS., DEC. 4-SUN., DEC. 7

Free except where indicated.

COUNTY

8:00-5:00— Old Mission at Santa Barbara

10:00-5:00— Mission Santa Ines at Solvang

10:00-5:00— La Purisima Mission State Historic Monument at Lompoc

Three Historic Spanish Missions, splendid work accomplished since 1925 in restoration. Special guides.

SANTA BARBARA—HISTORIC ADOBES.

9:00-5:00— Covarrubias, 715 Santa Barbara, Santa Barbara County Chamber of Commerce. Telephone 6189.

Headquarters Old Mission Days Committee

§Carrillo, 11 E. Carrillo, S. B. Foundation

§Casa de la Guerra, 15 East De la Guerra. Shops

§Orena, 39 East De la Guerra and adjoining.

*Miranda, 806 Anacapa, E. Sparrow

*El Cuartel, 122 E. Canon Perdido, Boy Scouts

*Ramirez, 935 Laguna, Mrs. A. L. M. Vhay

EXHIBITS

9:00-5:00— Museum of Natural History—Indian Artifacts

8:00-5:00— Old Mission.—Relics, historic manuscripts, 1784-1850

9:00-9:00— S. B. Public Library—Paintings and material relating to Spanish Period Store Windows

POINTS OF INTEREST

County Court House—Murals

9:00-5:00—§Lobero Theatre, 33 E. Canon Perdido

9:00-5:00—S. B. Botanic Garden—Mission Dam

Sunday—*2:00-5:00. §—Not Open.)—11:00-5:00.

SPECIAL EVENTS

TUESDAY, DEC. 2

10:00—ILLUSTRATED TALK, "Making a California Garden," E. D. Rowe, National Park Service. La Purisima, at Santa Barbara Public Library

THURSDAY, DEC. 4—Saint Barbara's Day

SANTA BARBARA—See Daily Program

10:00—HIGH MASS, Old Mission, celebrated by Fr. Patrick, O.F.M.

2:30—WILDFLOWER PLANTING on hill

3:00—SACRED CONCERT by PADRE CHORISTERS, Old Mission

Following LA TIRADA DEL BOLO, Scene from old-time christening, steps of Mission

7:30—ILLUSTRATED TALKS, "Beginnings of Santa Barbara Mission and Presidio," Fr. Augustine, O.F.M. and Owen O'Neill, Public Library

FRIDAY, DEC. 5

See Daily Program, Page 1

SANTA BARBARA—Special Events

2:00-4:30—RECEPTION at Covarrubias Adobe, 715 Santa Barbara. Hostesses—Civic Organizations, Spanish Families

7:30—BRIEF ILLUSTRATED TALKS, "Authentic Costumes of Early California" and "Early Days—Missions Santa Ines and La Purisima and Historic Ranches"—Santa Barbara Public Library

SATURDAY, DEC. 6

SANTA BARBARA—See Daily Program

2:00-4:30—RECEPTION at Covarrubias Adobe, Honoring National and State Park and other official visitors

6:45—OLD MISSION DAYS DINNER, Restaurante del Paseo. Distinguished speakers, Mexican entertainers

Make reservations by Fri., Dec. 5 at Chamber of Commerce, 715 Santa Barbara, phone 6189. $1.51 with taxes.

SOLVANG   Mission Santa Ines

10:00-5:00—CONDUCTED TOURS OF MISSION

2:00-4.30—RECEPTION. Hostesses from Santa Ynez Valley and N. D. G. W.

2:30—TALK, "History of Mission Santa Ines," Fr. Finnian Carroll, O.F.M. Cap, presiding

SUNDAY, DEC. 7

SANTA BARBARA—See Daily Program and Sunday Hours

2:00-4:30—RECEPTION, Covarrubias Adobe

3:00—SACRED CONCERT by PADRE CHORISTERS—Old Mission

LOMPOC   La Purisima Mission State Historic Monument

Celebrating 154th anniversary Dedication of first Mission at Lompoc. First service since 1836. Buildings restored since 1934 by Civilian Conservation Corps under direction National Park Service. One of finest and largest projects in country. Open to public daily 9:00-5:00.

10:00-5:00—CONDUCTED TOURS

11:00—SOLEMN MASS, celebrated by Fr. Augustine, Vice-Provincial O.F.M. St. Anthony's Choir. Unveiling presentation paintings and plaque marking burial of Fr. Fayeras, O.F.M.

12:30—LUNCHEON PERIOD

Visitors please bring box lunches. Hot coffee will be served in rear corridor. Official Guests with cards requested to meet at C.C.C. Mess Hall on hill, rear Mission.

1:45—ILLUSTRATED TALK in Chapel. Presiding Darwin Tate, Chief, Division of Beaches and Parks; "REBUILDING MISSION LA PURISIMA CONCEPCION," Earl P. Hanson

2:45—SACRED CONCERT—St. Anthony's Choir

For additional Programs, Information and Reservations please address Old Mission Days Committee, 715 Santa Barbara Street, Santa Barbara, Calif., telephone 6189.

visitors were leaving the church, news of the bombing of Pearl Harbor came to them through their automobile radios. Pearl Chase, a member of the La Purísima Advisory Committee and of the Old Mission Days Committee, wrote about it a few days afterward.

> The outbreak of war with Japan, announced on Sunday in the midst of the beautiful observance at our rebuilt Mission La Purísima Concepción, brought also the thought that what man's idealism has once created may be rebuilt.[20]

Mark Harrington wrote a note of appreciation for Old Mission Days to Pearl Chase on December 13, and also remembered his surprise at the war news.

> It was a dramatic moment when we came out of church and found that war had been forced upon us! Hoping that the Purísima project can continue, war or no war.[21]

Charles A. Storke, *Santa Barbara News-Press* publisher, and chair of the Old Mission Days Committee, wrote Chase that he felt positive about the event, despite the eclipsing news story.

> Personally, I am very enthusiastic over the results that were accomplished through Old Mission Days. It is unfortunate that the war broke as it did and robbed us of some of our best potential publicity. But I think, all in all, it was well worth the efforts that were put forth by everyone.[22]

Camp Cooke

Nine months before the beginning of World War II, Army personnel arrived in Lompoc to establish Camp Cooke.[23] This became the primary military installation in Santa Barbara County, guarding the Channel Islands shoreline and Ellwood Oil Fields against the imminently expected Japanese attack. When erecting Camp Cooke, military and National Park Service officials were given federal authority to dismantle the facilities of the Twin Camps for reuse in the new Army installation to be located on the other side of Lompoc, closer to the Pacific Ocean.[24] The portable wooden structures were disassembled and removed to Camp Cooke along with all Army vehicles and other components of the Twin Camps. The National Park Service retained its vehicles and other equipment, removing them

NEW DEAL ADOBE

CIVILIAN CONSERVATION CORPS

OFFICE OF THE DIRECTOR

WASHINGTON, D. C.

FILE REFERENCE:

Lompoc,California,February 19--20,1941.

Camp S.P.--29,Company 1951.

To The Director of CCC;
     Two companies occupy this camp site,SCS-9,
company 2950,and the above SP-29.
Buildings are of the fixed type,SP-29,were occupied for the first time,
July,1934,and continually occupied since that time.Buildings are in
splendid condition,and the camp in general,in excellent condition,and
greatly improved since my last inspection.Considerable rehabilitation
work completed since last visit,namely;rehabilitate mess-hall,re-crea-
tion-hall,infirmary,kitchen,store-room,wash-showers,educational build-
ing.All the above buildings present a splendid appearance with knotty-
pine,and tile in the kitchen.Latter,tile donated.
     Mess-lunches;One mess-hall -kitchen for the
two companies.Excellent setup-.Thoroughly experienced cooks.

     Morale; Excellent.About one half of the en-
rollees are of the Spanish-American type,and a very good lot of boys.

     Camp Administration;Captain Black with nearly
eight years in the CCC,is in general command of the two companies.
Has been in command since April,1940,and done an excellent job of it.
Company 1951 supervises the funds,etc covering the two camps on the
camp exchange.Net worth of all funds Co.,1951,Jan.31st.,$ 1.688.95.
Have a splendid Personnel throughout camp.

     Recreation;Not a problem in this camp.Enrollees
can go to Lompoc,two miles from camp week-ends,.Have one,well furnished
recreation-hall with three pool-tables,two ping-pong tables.Also have
an abundance of reading material,small games,and a splendid reading-
room.Also basket-ball,volley-ball,horse-shoes,archery,bad-minton,and
boxing.For religous ser vices can go to Lompoc every Sunday if they wish

     Work projects;Enrollees are very satisfactory,
alltho work projects,have been retarded,due to the exceedingly heavy
rains,and much lost time on that account.Co-operation,excellent.
Most of the trucks,Technical Service,are old models, and have outlived
their usefullness.In poor shape,and should be replaced.

     Shoes-clothing;Excellent condition.

     Subversive activities;None in camp.

     Except for few broken glass windows,old doors,
and door screens,camp in excellent condition.Might mention,these items
have been reguistioned.Have no showers in infirmary,and attach "Immediat
Action" memo for one.
    Yours very truly,
    M.J.Bowen,Special Investigator.

Inspection Report (1941).

[NATIONAL ARCHIVES, RECORD GROUP 35, WASHINGTON, D.C.]

FEDERAL SECURITY AGENCY

CIVILIAN CONSERVATION CORPS

OFFICE OF THE DIRECTOR

WASHINGTON, D.C.

Lompoc,California,October 6,1941.

FILE REFERENCE:

Camp S.P-29,Company 1951.

To The Director of CCC;
           Was a twin camp until recently,when one of
companies were sent to Camp Roberts.Now occupied by one company.
Fixed type buildings,construuted in 1934,and in need of some rehabilitation,particularly paint,flooring,doors,shower in Infirmary,and
electric wiring.(See "immediate action report attached).

           Morale; Good,alltho many enrollees leave camp,
get jobs,and do not return for the right kind of a discharge.The
usual follow system is in force,notifying selection agency,parents,
and enrollees.
           Mess; Good.No complaints.

           Camp Administration;Present Camp Commander
assumed command of the company last June,and has made very good
progress.Has had ten months CCC duty,but many years in the regular
Army.Very good Technical Personnel,and all on CCC duty for some years
Financial condition,very good. Net worth funds Sept.30th.$ 1.443.96.

           Camp recreation; Not a problem here,as camp
located about five miles from City of Lompoc,where the company has
very good Public relations.Have week-end trips to Lompoc.
Also have plenty reading material,radios,weekly movies,all camp nite,
numerous small games,and a good supply of athletic equipment.

           Work projects; Retarded at this time,due to
low company strength,and the fact,some fifty enrollees are on recreation buildings in Santa Monica,qassisting on construction work
for the Army.The latter have a side-camp in Sa nta Monica.
Co-operation,satisfactory.

           Shoes-clothing; All well supplied.

           Subversive activities;None in camp.

           Camp is clean,and good shape,considering age
of buildings,and the fact,some rehabilitation work needed.

           Yours very truly,

           M.J.Bowen,Special Investigator.

Inspection Report (1941).
[NATIONAL ARCHIVES, RECORD GROUP 35, WASHINGTON, D.C.]

to storehouses elsewhere in California for the duration of the war. Only two adobe residences constructed for camp military staff remained standing on the mesa behind the mission. They were left to serve as state park employee residences, as the twelve acres of former CCC terrain reverted to the scrub brush common to northern Santa Barbara County.

Camp Cooke served as an Army facility until September 1, 1956, when it was selected as an Intercontinental Ballistic Missile research and development facility.[25] In 1958, the installation was expanded and renamed Vandenberg Air Force Base.[26] The decades of military metamorphosis erased all physical evidence of the CCC presence.

Hageman after La Purísima

Fred Hageman produced a lengthy illustrated report on the architectural reconstruction of the mission, which he published on April 25, 1938.[27] He left the mission project shortly after Ed Negus, in 1939.[28] Because of his experience in adobe design, Hageman found work planning the Jameson Ranch and two adobes in Santa Ynez.[29] In early 1940, he was the architect for the reconstruction of the Miramar Hotel in Montecito.[30] During World War II, he worked for the Navy in Georgia designing boats,[31] and after the war he went into partnership with a Glendale, California builder, Frank W. Green.[32] They designed and built a shopping center as well as the Ford Agency Building in Glendale,[33] but were too far ahead of their time with the shopping center concept. It failed, and Hageman lost everything. Ed Negus discovered that Hageman began drinking.

> He met a bad end. He was go, go, go all the time and burned himself out. He and his wife Evelyn had no children and Martha and I couldn't keep up with him. He was very dynamic and was the force behind the reconstruction. If it hadn't been for him keeping track of the stuff and getting it figured out and contacting everybody, no one could have done it.[34]

On the evening of April 14, 1948, forty-three-year-old Fred Hageman ingested an overdose of the barbiturate Seconal and died at 3:30 A.M. in Glendale Sanitarium and Hospital on Thursday, April 15.[35] Despite this unhappy end to his life, Hageman can be appreciated today through the results of his work with the CCC enrollees at Mission La Purísima. Here his architectural skills, attention to detail, and enthusiasm are still apparent.

La Purísima Today

After the State of California's Division of Parks (later renamed Department of Parks and Recreation) assumed control and maintenance of the mission complex in 1941, more structures were gradually rebuilt. By 1988, ten of the thirteen mission buildings had been reconstructed. It was fitting that the California Conservation Corps, which came into existence in 1978 and inherited many of the policies and structure of the original CCC,[36] was contracted by the state to reconstruct the blacksmith shop and aqueduct in a historically accurate manner.

Today, a threatening change is working against La Purísima's pristine site in the Los Berros Canyon. Santa Barbara County's population mushroomed after World War II, and former agricultural lands in the Lompoc vicinity now provide more and more land for housing and commercial development. State staff are concerned about proposals to build nearby housing, thereby creating a modern intrusion on La Purísima's horizon. Surrounding development would destroy the mission's historically accurate appearance, an appearance that is the legacy of the labor of the Civilian Conservation Corps.

Before leaving the project in 1939, Fred Hageman wrote an appropriate conclusion to La Purísima's reconstruction.

> And so we come to the end of present reconstruction, and find that we have an imposing row of long, low, white adobe buildings, surmounted by broad expanses of red tiled roofs, extending nearly a thousand feet along a northeast-southwest axis, facing across the little canyon of Los Berros toward the Indian quarter. In front of the Church and beside the Shops and Quarters Building is the hard, bare plaza where Padre Payeras once assembled his hundreds of dusky children and instructed them in the orders of the day. While in front of the Residence Building the perfume from myriad flowers hangs heavy in the air, and the only sound we hear in the hush of an evening is the tinkling splash of the water in the fountains or perhaps the whirring wings of the scarlet-throated hummingbird as he gorges himself with nectar, unable to resist the lure of so enticing a display. Should we wonder, then, that we find this line written in the Visitors' Register by a descendant of a Spanish pioneer? "Gracias a Diós. La memoria vivirá." Thanks be to God. Its memory will live.[37]

1. Civilian Conservation Corps, Los Angeles District, *Official Annual,* Ninth Corps Area (Van Nuys, California, 1938), p. 119.
2. Ibid, p. 119.
3. Edward Negus Interview with Christine E. Savage, Lompoc, California, July 19, 1989.
4. H.V. Smith letter to Newton Drury, January 25, 1952, correspondence files, Mission La Purísima Archives, Lompoc, California.
5. CCC *Annual,* p. 119.
6. Dana Bartlett letter to H.V. Smith, November 12, 1940, correspondence files, Mission La Purísima Archives, Lompoc, California.
7. Ibid.
8. H.V. Smith letter to Inspector [first name unavailable] Clarke, October 29, 1940, correspondence files, Mission La Purísima Archives, Lompoc, California.
9. La Purísima Guest List for Old Mission Days, Mission La Purísima, "Pearl Chase Papers," Boxes 1-9, Community Development and Conservation Collection, Special Collections, Library, University of California at Santa Barbara.
10. Ibid.
11. Dana Bartlett letter to H.V. Smith, November 4, 1940, correspondence files, Mission La Purísima Archives, Lompoc, California.
12. H.V. Smith letter to Dana Bartlett, October 11, 1940, correspondence files, Mission La Purísima Archives, Lompoc, California.
13. Dana Bartlett letter to H.V. Smith, September 10, 1941, correspondence files, Mission La Purísima Archives, Lompoc, California.
14. Old Mission Days Program, October 29, 1941, La Purísima Mission, "Pearl Chase Papers," Boxes 1-9, Community Development and Conservation Collection, Special Collections, Library, University of California at Santa Barbara.
15. *Santa Barbara News-Press,* December 7, 1941, December 8, 1941, and December 9, 1941; *Lompoc Record,* December 5, 1941 and December 12, 1941.
16. *Lompoc Record,* December 5, 1941.
17. *Lompoc Record,* December 12, 1941.
18. *Lompoc Record,* December 5, 1941.
19. *Lompoc Record,* December 12, 1941.
20. Pearl Chase letter to H.L. Blaisdell, December 15, 1941, La Purísima Mission, "Pearl Chase Papers," Boxes 1-9, Community Development and Conservation Collection, Special Collections, Library, University of California at Santa Barbara.
21. Mark R. Harrington letter to Pearl Chase, December 13, 1941, La Purísima Mission, "Pearl Chase Papers," Boxes 1-9, Community Development and Conservation Collection, Special Collections, Library, University of California at Santa Barbara.
22. Charles A. Storke letter to Pearl Chase, December 23, 1941, La Purísima Mission, "Pearl Chase Papers," Boxes 1-9, Community Development and Conservation Collection, Special Collections, Library, University of California at Santa Barbara.
23. Tami Asire, "Camp Cooke Activity," *Lompoc Centennial,* published by the *Lompoc Record,* August 7, 1988.
24. United States Department of Agriculture, Forest Service, *CCC Administrative Handbook, Region 5* (Washington, D.C., October 1938), pp. 173-174 and 177.

25. First Strategic Aerospace Division, Vandenberg Air Force Base, *Launch: The Story of Vandenberg,* Boone Publications (Lubbock, Texas, 1970), p. 17.

26. Ibid.

27. Richard S. Whitehead, ed., *An Archaeological and Restoration Study of Mission La Purísima Concepción—Reports Written for the National Park Service by Fred C. Hageman and Russell C. Ewing,* Santa Barbara Trust for Historic Preservation (Santa Barbara, 1980), p. xiv.

28. Negus Interview.

29. Ibid.

30. *Santa Barbara News-Press,* February 25, 1940.

31. Negus Interview.

32. Russell Holmes Fletcher, ed., *Who's Who in California, 1942-43,* Vol. 1, Who's Who Publications (Los Angeles, 1943), p. 367.

33. Negus Interview.

34. Ibid.

35. Death Certificate No. 6516, Los Angeles County Hall of Records, Los Angeles, California.

36. Mercedes Azar, ed., *California Conservation Corps 1981 Annual Report,* California Conservation Corps, Secretary of Resources Agency, Office of the Governor (Sacramento, 1981), p. 8.

37. Frederick C. Hageman and Olaf T. Hagen, *Mission La Purísima Concepción—A Glance Through its History and the Story of its Restoration,* National Park Service, United States Department of the Interior (undated), Mission La Purísima Archives, Lompoc, California, p. 31.

For Further Reading

Baer, Kurt and Hugo Rudinger, *Architecture of the California Missions,* UC Press (Los Angeles, 1958).

Dearborn, Ned Harland, *Once in a Lifetime—Guide to the CCC Camp,* Charles Merrill Company (New York, 1936).

Engelhardt, Zephyrin, O.F.M. *Misión La Concepción Purísima de María Santísima,* Mission Santa Barbara (Santa Barbara, 1932).

Grower, Calvin W., "The Struggle of Blacks for Leadership Positions in the CCC, 1933-42," *Journal of Negro History,* April 1976; 61(2): pp. 123-35.

Holland, Kenneth and Frank Ernest Hill, *Youth in the CCC,* American Council on Education (Washington, 1942).

Hosmer, Charles B., Jr., *Preservation Comes of Age, Vol. II,* University Press of Virginia (Charlottesville, 1981).

Jernberg, Albert W., *My Brush Monkeys—A Narrative of the CCC,* Richard R. Smith Publishers (New York, 1941).

Lacy, Leslie Alexander, *The Soil Soldiers,* Chilton Book Company (Radnor, Pennsylvania, 1976).

Rauch, Basil, *The History of the New Deal, 1933-38,* Creative Age Press (New York, 1944).

Salmond, John A., *The Civilian Conservation Corps, 1933-42: A New Deal Case Study,* Duke University Press (Durham, NC, 1967).

Sandos, James A., "Levantamiento! The 1824 Chumash Uprising," *The Californians,* Vol. 5, No. 1 (Jan.-Feb. 1987).

Sunset Editors, *The California Missions,* Lane Publishing Company (Menlo Park, California, 1979).

Swain, Donald C., "The National Park Service and the New Deal, 1933-40" *Pacific Historical Review,* Vol. XLI, No. 3 (August 1972), pp. 312-332.

Thomas, David Hurst, ed., *Columbian Consequences,* Vol. 1, Smithsonian Institution Press (Blue Ridge Summit, Pennsylvania, 1989).

Whitehead, Richard S., ed., *An Archaeological and Restoration Study of Mission La Purísima Concepción—Reports Written for the National Park Service by Fred C. Hageman and Russell C. Ewing,* Santa Barbara Trust for Historic Preservation (Santa Barbara, 1980).

Wilkinson, S. Kristina and Michael R. Hardwick, "La Purísima, A Living Museum of Spanish Colonial History," *Noticias,* Santa Barbara Historical Society, Vol. 19, No. 2 (Summer, 1973), pp. 1-9.

Wirth, Conrad L., *The Civilian Conservation Corps Program of the United States Department of the Interior,* March 1933 to June 30, 1943, U.S. Department of the Interior (Chicago, 1944).